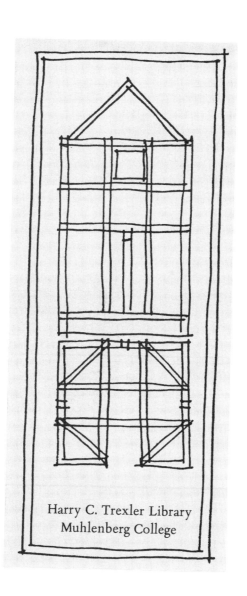

TECHNOLOGY AND
U.S. COMPETITIVENESS

Recent Titles in
Contributions in Economics and Economic History

Cities in the World-System
Reşat Kasaba, editor

The Economics of Intellectual Property in a World Without Frontiers: A Study of Computer Software
Meheroo Jussawalla

Reforming Financial Systems: Policy Changes and Privatization
Neal Zank, John A. Mathieson, Frank T. Neidar, Kathleen D. Vickland, and Ronald J. Ivey

Managing Modern Capitalism: Industrial Renewal and Workplace Democracy in the United States and Western Europe
M. Donald Hancock, John Logue, and Bernt Schiller, editors

Corporate Networks and Corporate Control: The Case of the Delaware Valley
Ralph M. Faris

Night Boat to New England, 1815-1900
Edwin L. Dunbaugh

Income and Inequality: The Role of the Service Sector in the Changing Distribution of Income
Cathy Kassab

Rural Change in the Third World: Pakistan and the Aga Khan Rural Support Program
Mahmood Hasan Khan and Shoaib Sultan Khan

Soviet Political Economy in Transition: From Lenin to Gorbachev
A. F. Dowlah

The Diary of Rexford G. Tugwell: The New Deal, 1932-1935
Edited by Michael Vincent Namorato

Making Markets: An Interdisciplinary Perspective on Economic Exchange
Robin Cantor, Stuart Henry, and Steve Rayner

TECHNOLOGY AND U.S. COMPETITIVENESS

An Institutional Focus

Edited by
W. Henry Lambright
and
Dianne Rahm

Prepared under the auspices of the Policy Studies Organization
Stuart S. Nagel, *Publications Coordinator*

Contributions in Economics and Economic History,
Number 139

Greenwood Press
New York • Westport, Connecticut • London

Library of Congress Cataloging-in-Publication Data

Technology and U.S. competitiveness : an institutional focus / edited
by W. Henry Lambright and Dianne Rahm : prepared under the auspices
of the Policy Studies Organization.
p.   cm. — (Contributions in economics and economic history,
ISSN 0084–9235 ; no. 139)
Includes bibliographical references and index.
ISBN 0–313–28560–8
1. Technological innovations—Economic aspects—United States.
2. Technology and state—United States. 3. Research, Industrial-
Government policy—United States. 4. Technology transfer.
5. Competition, International. I. Lambright, W. Henry, 1939-
II. Rahm, Dianne. III. Policy Studies Organization. IV. Title:
Technology and US competitiveness. V. Series.
HC110.T4T395   1992
338′.064′0973—dc20   92–8845

British Library Cataloguing in Publication Data is available.

Library of Congress Catalog Card Number: 92–8845
ISBN: 0–313–28560–8
ISSN: 0084–9235

First published in 1992

Greenwood Press, 88 Post Road West, Westport, CT 06881
An imprint of Greenwood Publishing Group, Inc.

Printed in the United States of America

The paper used in this book complies with the
Permanent Paper Standard issued by the National
Information Standards Organization (Z39.48-1984).

10 9 8 7 6 5 4 3 2 1

Contents

Introduction

W. Henry Lambright and Dianne Rahm

One of the more critical issues on the U.S. policy agenda is that of "technology and competitiveness." Virtually all nations see their economic futures linked to technology. States sponsor science and technology ventures to aid their competitiveness vis-a-vis one another. The U.S. government worries about technology in terms of Japan and Europe. The former Soviet Union republics and other nations wish to acquire technology that will develop their civilian economies. Without a doubt, technology and competitiveness have arrived as items on the world's agenda. Within the United States, the question is what is to be done about the issue. Competitiveness is a concept that hits hard at the American people in terms of jobs, income, and quality of life. It contributes to a sense of well-being and optimism about the future. It can also provide a basis for malaise and pessimism.

In the White House and elsewhere technology and competitiveness is a controversial issue. Its problem is that there are those who equate it with "industrial policy," and industrial policy goes against the grain of conservative, market-oriented ideology. Also, there is fear that the government does not do well when it intervenes in the economy so as to help certain technologies while (inevitably) neglecting others. The fact that many other industrial democracies do so is ignored or played down.

Yet the global economy is real and is not likely to go away. National economies do not exist in isolation any more. Technological developments in one country immediately impact the scientific, industrial, and political base of rivals around the world. In response to this, the White House cautiously does what it might wish not to do: It moves into programs involving the development and application of new technologies with an aim to compete better industrially. The process is slow, tortuous, and often denied. It is politically possible to talk about technology and competitiveness, as long as this is distinguished from industrial policy. In typical U.S. fashion, we are at present "muddling through" to a technology policy linked to industrial competitiveness.

How did we get to this point? Where are we going? What do the chapters in this volume have to contribute to the present policy discussion?

GETTING TO TODAY

The remarkable fact about technology and competitiveness is that it is not so new. One can go back to the U.S. Constitution with its patent clause and the policies of Alexander Hamilton to see how founding leaders were concerned about the economic competitiveness and the infant industries of the new nation. They wanted to fully free the United States from its status as a political colony. They knew that unless the nation developed an indigenous industrial base, it would be economically dependent on the old world.

Hence, a great deal of early domestic policy was geared to interstate commerce, internal improvements such as canal and road building, and even education. This policy had its roots in a desire to provide economic autonomy to the new nation. The establishment of land-grant agricultural colleges in the mid-ninteenth century was a case of federal policy linking technology to a particular economic sector of the society. After the Civil War, the federal government subsidized the railroad industry. Shipping technology created new developments in steel ships, coal engines, and canals, requiring enormous engineering skills. By this time, the country was increasingly independent vis-a-vis Europe, and was continuing to promote domestic economic development and other values by exploiting new technology.

Long before anyone coined the current term—dual-use technology—the airplane was seen as having both military and civilian uses. A new technology agency—the National Advisory Committee on Aeronautics (NACA)—was added to the federal structure in 1915 to perform research and development (R&D) on this new technology. That it did, for decades, much to the benefit of both the military and civilian aviation industries. NACA was incorporated into the National Aeronautics and Space Administration (NASA) in 1958.

The depression gave rise to a great deal of rhetoric about government's stimulating invention and industry, but relatively little in the way of concrete programs. The emergency was so grave that government policy was geared much more to the here and now than to the creation of new technology-based industry. During World War II, of course, the only technology policy that mattered was winning the war.

After the war, however, the United States turned to ways government might "commercialize" some of the technologies spawned during the conflict. The principal thrust came with civilian atomic energy. Could this great invention, used only to kill people, be turned toward their benefit? If the United States did not try to do so, it was clear that other nations possessing nuclear expertise would. Hence, during the 1950s, the federal attempt to develop and deploy the "peaceful atom" was prodigious. In the 1960s, civilian nuclear power "arrived" as a commercially viable technology. Indeed, there are those today who believe the lessons of federal technology policy are essentially negative—because of government's promotion of civilian nuclear power.

In the 1960s the dominant federal focus, however, was not nuclear power as much as it was space and aeronautics. In space, there was a remarkable success story: the development and deployment of communications satellites. We so take them for granted today that we forget they did not exist before NASA worked with industry, and especially the COMSAT Corporation (created by Congress for this purpose) to put them to commercial use. Ironically, also in the 1960s, came a failure in technology policy. The United States, in competition with the British and French, launched the Supersonic Transport (SST) project. The aim was to develop the world's fastest commercial airplane. Sonic booms, economic problems, and growing political opposition led to the cancellation of this particular federal venture in 1971. The British-French Concorde flew, but never achieved the commercial objectives contemplated.

In the 1970s came the energy crisis and a host of federal attempts to develop and commercialize new energy sources, such as solar energy and synthetic fuels. Also, the Carter administration spoke of "reinventing the automobile," the aim being to help the U.S. automobile industry compete better with the Japanese. These programs and proposed efforts were cut back severely or largely abandoned in the 1980s by the Reagan administration. Labeling these energy ventures as failures, and many ideas about reinvigorating civilian industry inappropriate, the Reagan administration approached federal technology policy conservatively. What federal technology policy there was, was highly specific, such as in relation to computers or high-temperature superconductivity. More often than not, the principal funder was the Defense Department. The policy focus was market oriented and reactive.

Ironically, it was during the 1980s, when the federal government did relatively little in a direct way, that the states moved forward and established proactive policies for S&T-based (science and technology) economic development. Indeed, from a standpoint of technology policy, the states were the leaders of policy innovation in the 1980s.

THE 1990s

In the present decade, the federal government is caught between the pressures presented by unrelenting international competition and domestic economic downturn on the one hand; and a conservative White House and huge budget deficit on the other. There is simply not much room to maneuver, especially when one party controls the presidency and another the Congress. Moreover, as this historical review suggests, while there is ample precedent for federal technology policies, these precedents are not unalloyed success stories. Mistakes can be and have been made, and these can be costly. The SST and synfuels programs were billion-dollar failures. Whether civilian nuclear power is an example that is positive or negative depends on one's point of view. Certainly, agriculture, aviation, and communications satellites are successful cases of federal technology policy. And we have not mentioned all the indirect examples of civilian technology that have come from military and space ventures—spin-offs that bolstered and accelerated the U.S. computer industry.

The past, however, very much represents a piecemeal approach to civilian technology policy. What is seen by many observers as necessary today is something much more comprehensive. There have been a number of studies about "strategic technologies"—a cluster of new capabilities that give promise to create the industries of the twenty-first century. Who will make the most (get the most) from these technologies?

That depends on decisions made today. There are those who worry that other nations—particularly the Japanese and Europeans—are making decisions, while the United States sits inertly by, waiting for someone else to lead. There is much evidence that even when the United States is first to invent, it still winds up lagging when it comes to technological deployment. Industrial sectors in which the United States has led have been lost or are in jeopardy. What happens when the country is slower than competitors to act on the new technologies? What is/should be the federal role?

The old piecemeal and largely reactive technology policies were geared to a world in which the United States was the dominant economic power from the standpoint of science, technology, and industry. The world of today and tomorrow is much more pluralistic. Moreover, other nations take technology and competitiveness very seriously. The United States is beginning to do so, with state and federal governments charting programs. Ironically, in the 1990s, with its economic downturn, there is difficulty—especially in the states—in maintaining some of the pioneering efforts in this field. Does this country have the administrative infrastructure in terms of agencies, programs, and astute leaders to make more correct than incorrect choices in terms of national investments and technology strategies?

It would seem that the U.S. response to the "new world order" of technology and competitiveness is just now emerging. What shape it will take remains to be seen. The chapters in this volume will add to the intellectual ferment now shaping U.S. technology policy.

THE ORGANIZATION OF THE BOOK

The authors contributing to this volume come at these issues from various vantage points. The chapters have been arrayed in terms of emphasizing federal, state, and more general policy perspectives.

Dianne Rahm's Chapter 1 deals with federal competitiveness policy. She tracks the past ten years of federal activity in the technology competitiveness field. In contrast to what many critics allege, she says there was a competitiveness policy in the Reagan years. It was largely an indirect, some might say minimalist, policy, but it was a policy nonetheless. It focused on what she calls "three basics: reduction of antitrust prosecution, increasing technology transfer, and precompetitive R&D cooperation." She examines this policy, along with the Bush administration approach. She sees policies becoming more pragmatic than during the predecessor regime, with "programs and institutions in flux."

In Chapter 2 Brack Brown is concerned with the bearing on competitiveness of federal efforts to stimulate the development and transfer of new technologies here and abroad. He notes that this policy contrasts with that to impede the transfer of new technology to foreign adversaries of the United States. How can federal policy promote and impede technology transfer at the same time? This dilemma is discussed, showing the complexities of balancing different interests in the present post-Cold War era.

Robert Chapman and Curt Reimann address the role of the National Institute of Standards and Technology (NIST) in connection with the competitiveness issue, in Chapter 3. NIST was built on the National Bureau of Standards and has a mission to work closely with industry. Chapman and Reimann discuss the R&D mission of NIST and how that relates to industrial competitiveness and especially note how NIST has sought to raise the level of quality in U.S. industry.

James Ball also takes an institutional focus, looking at the nation's largest agency concerned with science and technology spending: the Department of Defense (DOD). In Chapter 4, Ball says DOD necessarily thinks fundamentally about military competitiveness; however, in the present era, it is aware that it has a stake in the economic strength of the nation. Ball examines the technology transfer effort of DOD. "Is it possible to beat defense swords into plowshares and convert defense technology into civilian applications?" The answer is "yes" according to Ball, who details how this is done and with what consequences.

With respect to state perspectives on these issues, W. Henry Lambright, Albert Teich, and Mark O'Gorman review the growth and present turbulence afflicting state efforts in technology-based economic development. In Chapter 5 they show that many of these programs were born in the early 1980s when states sought to use technology to diversify their economies. In the early 1990s, hit by severe budget stress, a number of states cut back on these technology initiatives. The chapter also discusses the relation (or nonrelation) of federal policies and state policies in this area.

Arthur Levine deals, from a state perspective, with an area of policy dominated by the federal government. In Chapter 6 he finds 35 states involved in space technology and related activities that have a bearing on U.S. competitiveness. There is even an Aerospace States Association. Types of state programs include spaceports, teleports, space research with commercial applications, and incentives to attract and retain space-related industries. Local governments are frequently involved in some of these ventures. Levine argues that the research programs are those most likely to impact on U.S. competitiveness.

Linda Parker has also written about state programs. However, in Chapter 7 she concentrates on the relatively fundamental research components of state activity. This effort, like other state science and technology programs, has been stimulated of late by the drive for economic development at the state level. Her interest is the problem of how to evaluate these programs. Do they work or not? Her chapter examines why confusion exists and ways program evaluation might be approached.

Other writers discuss technology and competitiveness from more general perspectives. In Chapter 8 Irwin Feller deals with technology and competitiveness from the angle of economic theory and organizational design. Feller traces the theoretical components of recent attempts to match government programs with civilian technologies. He finds a fundamental weakness in the lack of an organizational framework to connect the numerous ad hoc components of U.S. technology policy.

Maria Papadakis' Chapter 9 on U.S. technology-based competitiveness policies illustrates the seeming inevitability of the current "competitiveness crisis," especially as it relates to Japan. The technology gap favoring the United States after World War II has eroded. She discusses the reasons Japan has competed so well vis-a-vis the United States in recent years. She sees Japan's manufacturing base as key, and Japan's policies to couple R&D with manufacturing technology in a way the U.S. finds quite difficult as especially important.

Sally Rood and Andee Rappazzo in Chapter 10 examine the relationship between organizational culture and competitiveness programs. Emphasizing implementation, they suggest that policy efforts might be more successful if details of specific firm behaviors were considered more carefully by policy formulators.

All these writers believe technology and U.S. competitiveness is a serious issue, badly in need of attention. The intent of these chapters is to contribute to the present debate, in the interest of enriching analysis and improving policy. The editors wish to thank the Section on Science and Technology in Government of the American Society for Public Administration for its support and encouragement.

I Federal Programs, Institutions, and Issues

1 Federal Competitiveness Policy: Programs and Institutions in Flux

Dianne Rahm

Competitiveness became an important issue more than a decade ago when it was recognized that the United States had failed to keep pace with other advanced industrialized nations. The root of the problem was—and still is—believed to lie in the inability of industry to capitalize on advances in science and technology. It was in the late stages of the Carter administration when the U.S. economic decline became clear. A consensus developed regarding the need to reinvigorate the private sector through increased research and development, which would result in more competitive products and manufacturing processes.

Recognizing the problem, the Reagan administration enacted policies on competitiveness. These policies, remaining within the parameters of the conservative ideological framework of the administration, had one common theme: offering government assistance to the private sector by allowing or participating in "precompetitive" collaboration. During the Bush administration there has been a modification of U.S. competitiveness policy. Reacting to dramatic changes in world politics (the ending of the Cold War and the Persian Gulf War), persistent economic distress, and a determined Congress, President Bush has been led reluctantly to support the development of "technology policy." This technology or industrial policy is less conservative than Reagan-era policy in large part because it emphasizes the appropriateness of greater government involvement in all stages of product and process R&D. Technology policy is controversial because it implies government overriding (or interfering with) free market processes through national strategic planning and targeting particular technologies for development.

This chapter will briefly review the main thrusts of competitiveness efforts during the 1980s and early 1990s. The first section will discuss why competitiveness became and why it has remained a national issue. The initial approach to international competitiveness adopted primarily during the Reagan era will be discussed in the next section. The focus will be on the central themes of reduction of antitrust prosecution, increasing technology transfer, and precompetitive R&D cooperation. Changes in competitiveness policies during the Bush administration will be addressed in the final section. Concentration will be on the identification of critical technologies, the switching role of the Department of Defense, and congressional leadership in development of U.S. technology policy.

COMPETITIVENESS AS A NATIONAL ISSUE

What is "competitiveness" and how did it become a national issue? Some background information will serve to highlight the main areas of importance.

The appropriateness of government investment in S&T or R&D has traditionally been unquestioned when the technology was for military or national defense purposes. Additionally, academic research done in the 1950s suggested a link between investment in civilian R&D and overall national economic prosperity. This relationship, while complicated and not clearly understood, has been—and continues to be—accepted by most government leaders.

The theory states that there will be an underinvestment in basic research in the private sector because no one firm will be able to fully expropriate profits resulting from basic research discoveries. The society as a whole, however, would gain from investment in basic research. The government, according to the theory, should intervene in this "market failure" and fund basic research. The federal government and most state governments—based largely on acceptance of this argument—fund a considerable array of S&T and R&D activities (Lambright and Rahm 1991; Rahm and Luce 1992).

While the funding rationalization may seem straightforward, problems arise in implementation. How do public officials distinguish basic research from other forms of research? What is the dividing line between basic and applied research or between applied research and development? When is a technology sufficiently developed so that it may be released to the market without continued government intervention? These are important considerations because economic theory suggests that firms can and do derive profits from applied research and development efforts—which is to say no market failure exists in those stages of R&D. If that is the case, then government funding in those phases may be nothing more than a direct taxpayer subsidy to specific industries.

The political or economic justification for government R&D assistance to specific industries has never been firmly rooted. Nevertheless, the perception of a widespread foreign practice of national support during all stages of R&D, coupled with the success of those foreign industries in U.S. markets, has resulted in a new political awareness. Loss of profitability of domestic firms vis-a-vis foreign industrial competitors (particularly Japanese firms) has resulted in reexamination of U.S. policy and a willingness on the part of legislators to intervene. In large part, emerging U.S. competitiveness policy seeks to emulate the activities of Japan's successful Ministry for International Trade and Industry (MITI) or the European industrial R&D promotion efforts known as ESPRIT and EUREKA (Marshall 1991b; Norris 1983). The question has become not if the government should support industrial R&D, but how and to what extent. The policy that depicts those relationships is called competitiveness or, by some, technology (or industrial) policy.

The perceived success of foreign countries has been tied to several rudimentary components. Among these are interfirm cooperation, long-term planning, government coordination and selection of technological priorities, and high levels of government support for civilian R&D. During the last decade, the United States has begun to consider these issues and has enacted policy with the goal of improving the competitive position of U.S. industry.

DEVELOPMENT OF A NATIONAL COMPETITIVENESS POLICY

During the eight years of the Reagan administration, and the early Bush administration, a national competitiveness policy emerged. It drew heavily from the Japanese example, which was seen as quite successful. The administration sought to provide mechanisms within the U.S. market system that would allow Japanese-style cooperation. To this end, three key themes of the Reagan-era competitiveness policy were: reduction of antitrust prosecution, increasing technology transfer from government labs to industry, and fostering "precompetitive" R&D collaboration.

Before 1980, the level of R&D cooperation amounted to little more than a handful of successful research parks, government funding of agricultural experiment stations, government support to land grant universities, and a few innovative national laboratory arrangements. During the Reagan years, thousands of organizational and institutional arrangements developed that, although they differed in detail, shared the common focus of cooperation.

The policy attempted to link industry with universities and government as well as to lower barriers to interfirm cooperation. Federal encouragement of cooperative R&D included efforts to transfer technologies developed in the national laboratories to industry, loosening patent and licensing restrictions for technologies developed fully or partially at taxpayer expense, becoming a partner in R&D with universities or industries, reducing the threat of antitrust prosecution for collaborating firms, and coordinating national cooperative efforts.

Within the United States a great variety of cooperative arrangements developed. Cooperative agreements among several firms, for instance, resulted in the evolution of Research and Development Limited Partnerships (RDLPs). Trilogy, for example, spread the risk of research across many manufacturers in an effort to facilitate further research (Murray 1981). Many joint ventures also emerged such as Microelectronics and Computer Technology Corporation (MCC), jointly formed by more than a dozen computer manufacturers, and Semiconductor Research Corporation (SRC), a joint effort of IBM, Hewlett-Packard, and Intel (Krieger 1987).

Technology transfer efforts, especially through licensing or direct transfer of government patents, resulted in new forms of cooperation between government labs and the private sector. The Solar Energy Research Institute (SERI), for instance, is a federal lab opened in 1977 with a clear mandate to share its research accomplishments with the private sector. SERI is working cooperatively with Spire Corporation on a program to develop cheaper photovoltaics (silicon cells that convert sunlight to electricity). If the research yields any commercializable results, Spire will hold the patent with the exclusive right to profit from research funded at least in part at taxpayer expense (Finegan 1987). Another instance of cooperation between the federal laboratories and industry can be seen in the agreement between IBM and Brookhaven National Laboratory. Brookhaven, which houses the nation's first large-scale synchrotron, permits IBM to use the device for research in X-ray lithography (a promising direction of research for increasing computer chip performance). Brookhaven also shares the synchrotron with about 90 academic and industrial R&D groups working on a variety of projects (Guterl 1987).

During the developmental stage of competitiveness policy, the federal government established within the National Science Foundation (NSF) both Engineering Research Centers (ERCs) and later on Science and

Technology Research Centers. The ERCs are government-university-industry partnerships doing directed basic research in newly emerging technologies (Gannes 1988). In 1989 the Science and Technology Research Centers were added with the notion of extending collaboration to more areas of basic science (Palca 1990).

Sematech is another example of federal cooperative R&D effort. Sematech is a research organization jointly funded by the federal government and a 14-member consortium of semiconductor manufacturers (U.S. Congress, 1988). Sharing funding and spreading the risk across several vendors, Sematech—which is short for semiconductor manufacturing technology—hopes to jump-start the U.S. chip industry. The government funding comes from the Pentagon, which has a national security interest in maintaining a domestic manufacturer of state-of-the-art chips for military systems.

The Reagan administration also created the Presidential Commission on Industrial Competitiveness by Executive Order 12428 in June 1983. The membership of the Commission was to be drawn from government, industry, and universities. The responsibility of the Commission was to advise the president on the "means of increasing the long-term competitiveness of United States industries at home and abroad, with particular emphasis on high-technology" (Reagan 1984).

In addition to creating new organizations, many laws were passed during the Reagan years. Central to federal efforts were attempts to streamline patent and licensing procedures (especially regarding technology transfer of federally developed technologies), and reduced antitrust prosecution to enable multifirm cooperation.

The first major policy initiative promoting cooperative R&D came with the Stevenson-Wydler Technology Innovation Act of 1980. Developed in large part during the Carter administration, the act sought to promote cooperation among academia, federal laboratories, labor, and industry. The act recognized that "government antitrust, economic, trade, patent, procurement, regulatory, research and development, and tax policies have significant impacts upon industrial innovation and development of technology" and that "no comprehensive national policy exists to enhance technological innovation for commercial and public purposes." The Stevenson-Wydler Act was the first attempt to establish such a policy.

The act directed the secretary of Commerce to establish and maintain an Office of Industrial Technology with the purpose of fostering innovation and improving U.S. technological competitiveness. Further, the act established Centers for Industrial Technology to be affiliated with universities or nonprofit institutions. These centers were to advance technological innovation by stimulating the interaction of individuals from industry and universities in cooperative technological development, and to support the continued development of a "generic research base . . . in which individual firms have little incentive to invest" but which has "significant economic or strategic importance."

Provisions of the act also allowed for the establishment of Offices of Research and Technology Applications (ORTA) in each of the federal laboratories with the purpose of transferring nationally developed technology to state and local governments and private industry. In conjunction, a Center for the Utilization of Federal Technology was established within the Commerce Department to serve as a clearinghouse for the transmission of information about federally owned or developed technologies to the states or private sector for utilization.

At the start of the Bush administration, the National Competitiveness Technology Transfer Act of 1989 was passed to amend and strengthen the technology transfer provisions of Stevenson-Wydler concerning government-owned contractor-operated national laboratories. This act was part of the National Defense Authorization Act for Fiscal Years 1990 and 1991.

Although on the surface the Stevenson-Wydler Act did much to promote cooperative R&D, problems emerged when the act ran into conflict with standing laws. For example, one of its major flaws rested with the handling of patent rights. The act did not specify who, in a cooperative agreement, was to get the rights to an invention, only that the parties must agree upon that matter before entering into relationships. The act also called for the Centers to be self-supporting and suggested that royalties be used either for the "compensation of the inventor or for the educational and research purposes of the Center." Since the Centers were to be self-supporting, the clearest avenue for royalties seemed to use them for the support of the Centers. But lacking the incentive of profit, industry and private inventors had little motive to become involved. The provisions for the sharing of federal technology also ran into difficulties, with the lack of adequate support among the labs for ORTAs and lack of commitment to technology transfer activities in general (Rahm et al. 1988).

Awareness of the problems associated with patents and trademarks led to the passage of the Bayh-Dole Act of 1980. This act stated that the policy of Congress was to use the patent system to promote the utilization of inventions flowing from federally funded research and to foster cooperation between universities, government, and industry. Under the act, small businesses and nonprofit organizations receiving money from the federal government (either in the form of a grant, contract, or cooperative agreement) could file for patent rights for an invention developed using federal money. The government, however, still retained "march-in rights," which allowed the federal agency under whose funding the invention was developed to mandate to the title holder that a license (exclusive, partially exclusive, or nonexclusive) must be given to a party of the agency's choice. The act also specified that organizations receiving a patent could not grant licenses to any firm unless the firm agreed to manufacture in the United States.

Small business, often argued to be the engine of U.S. innovation, was the target of the Small Business Innovation Development Act of 1982, which sought to direct the flow of federal monies to small industries. The act called for the Small Business Innovation Research program (SBIR), which required that government agencies with extramural R&D budgets target 0.2 to 1.25 percent of their budgets specifically for small business.

Further attempts to elaborate the nature of industry-government cooperative agreements came with the next amendment to the patent laws. In the Trademark Clarification Act of 1984, industrial firms involved in cooperative agreements with federal labs or receiving federal money for R&D work were restricted to two years in which to apply for title to the invention. If no such application was made, then the government could try to transfer the technology to another interested party and thus foster the commercialization of technologies developed at taxpayer expense.

Although the initiatives so far discussed deal primarily with the interaction of firms with government R&D facilities, the federal legislation of the last decade has not been silent on the issue of interfirm cooperative R&D. One of the major determinants of the willingness of firms to participate in joint research rests with the level of enforcement of antitrust laws. It is not surprising that fear of antitrust prosecution, with mandated harsh penalties, would keep firms from cooperating with other firms in R&D plans.

To remedy this, Congress established the "Rule of Reason Standard" for cooperative R&D in the National Cooperative Research Act of 1984. The rule was not unlike the rule of reason established by the Supreme Court in the famous 1911 Standard Oil Company dissolution case, which specified that not all combinations ought to be considered in restraint of trade and that the government ought to confine its concerns to those instances where there was an "unreasonable" restraint of trade. So too, the National Cooperative Research Act specified that in any action under the antitrust laws, the conduct of persons or firms entering into cooperative or joint research efforts should be judged on the basis of the reasonableness of the coalition. The act was intended to encourage firms to enter into joint research efforts and to eliminate one of the factors that had prevented such activity.

The National Cooperative Research Act provided for the elimination of the standard triple damages in the event of a suit. By providing for only single damages and attorney's fees, the act discouraged litigation (Zwart 1987). The ease of providing for single damages in the event of prosecution is another essential feature of the law. Just by registering cooperative research programs with the U.S. Federal Trade Commission and the Justice Department, any future antitrust challenges are automatically restricted to actual damages suffered (Glassie 1987).

Another legislative initiative supportive of cooperative R&D came just two years later. The Federal Technology Transfer Act of 1986 encouraged all government-operated laboratories to engage in cooperative research arrangements with other federal labs, state and local governments, industry, universities, and nonprofit agencies. But, most important, the act eliminated a restriction on patents that had been a problem up to this point. The act declared that any federal laboratory could, in advance, agree to grant patent rights to any collaborating party that desired them. This removed one large obstacle for industrial involvement with federal labs.

The Federal Laboratory Consortium for Technology Transfer was also established by the Federal Technology Transfer Act. This consortium was designed to educate industry, universities, nonprofit agencies, and federal labs alike as to the advantages of utilizing federal technology.

The Omnibus Trade and Competitiveness Act of 1988 contained a separate section dealing exclusively with competitiveness. Title V, Subtitle B is called the Technology Competitiveness Act. This legislation had several far-reaching purposes. First, the act renamed the National Bureau of Standards to the National Institute of Standards and Technology and reorganized that agency to increase its "ability to enhance the competitiveness of American industry while maintaining its traditional function as lead national laboratory for providing the measurements, calibrations, and quality assurance techniques" for industry. Second, the act sought "to assist private sector initiatives to capitalize on advanced technology." Third, the act promised "to advance, through cooperative efforts among industries, universities, and government laboratories, promising research and development projects which can be optimized by the private sector for commercial and industrial applications." Finally, the act proposed to "promote shared risks, accelerated development, and pooling of skills which will be necessary to strengthen America's manufacturing industries."

The National Institute of Standards and Technology was directed under the law to perform research in engineering, math, statistics, computer science, materials science, and the physical sciences to assist industry in technological development and facilitate commercialization of new products and processes. The Omnibus Trade and Competitiveness Act also provided for the establishment of Regional Centers for the Transfer of Manufacturing Technology to be affiliated with nonprofit organizations that apply for government financing. These Regional Centers are to serve as the transfer mechanisms by which technologies developed at the Institute can be spread to manufacturing organizations. Specifically targeted areas for research and transfer include automated manufacturing systems and process technologies.

Aside from establishing a clearinghouse for dissemination of technological information to states and local governments, the act also established the Advanced Technology Program with a mission to assist business in the application of generic technologies and research both to refine manufacturing techniques and to develop new commercial products. The Advanced Technology Program is granted by law the latitude to aid U.S. joint research efforts both through advice and participation. Participation might include partial start-up funding, assuming a minority share of the operational costs for up to five years, and making available equipment, facilities, and personnel.

Although legal statutes have had a strong influence, Reagan-era competitiveness initiatives were also implemented through presidential order. Prior to the passage of the National Cooperative Research Act, which provided for a waiver of triple damages for approved R&D enterprises, there was widespread industrial and entrepreneur hesitation to risk such expensive litigations. To overcome such hesitation and encourage industrial cooperation, the Reagan administration embarked on a controversial reinterpretation of the antitrust rules. Some of these changes were incorporated into the National Cooperative Research Act of 1984, but others were changes of overall antitrust enforcement policy rather than changes of legal statute.

The Justice Department began the reinterpretation with its 1980 clarification of guidelines for antitrust prosecution. Joint research projects were to be left alone if they adhered to the spirit of cooperative research—the research activity was of too great a scale for one individual firm to undertake the research independently, the research was long-term and of broad scope, the joint research agreement did not prohibit individual firms from independently researching the same project, and the results of the research would not be used to suppress industrywide advancement (Ewing 1980).

The complex and subjective nature of interpretation of the rules led the Justice Department to issue a pamphlet with guidelines for possible antitrust prosecutions concerning joint ventures. The pamphlet contained examples of how Justice would deal with specific cases. The Justice Department also invited firms to have their joint research plans reviewed by the antitrust division prior to implementation of an agreement and to inform the firms if Justice would issue a challenge to such collaboration (Ewing 1981).

Following the new guidelines, Justice took no action against the dozen-member consortium of computer firms that established Microelectronics and Computer Technology Corporation in 1982, despite the fact that these members included many of the big computer manufacturers such as Control Data Corporation, Digital Equipment Corporation, and Honeywell. Nor did Justice contest the formation of Semiconductor Research Corporation by IBM, Hewlett-Packard, and Intel.

The direction of loosening of antitrust enforcement has been continued by the House of Representatives. In June 1990, the House voted to expand the relaxation of antitrust prosecutions first begun under the National Cooperative Research Act of 1984. The House bill, the National Cooperative Production Amendments of 1990, seeks to remove the triple damages for antitrust violations in manufacturing so that joint ventures would be more attractive to industry (Tolchin 1990). The Senate has yet to consider the bill.

From this discussion, it can be seen that during the developmental period of U.S. competitiveness policy, the emphasis was placed on the reduction of antitrust prosecution, increasing technology transfer, and fostering precompetitive R&D collaborative efforts. Changes in the world situation, however, caused a shift in competitiveness policy during the Bush administration.

MODIFICATIONS OF NATIONAL COMPETITIVENESS POLICY

A number of significant world changes have occurred since the beginning of the Bush administration, including the Persian Gulf War, the end of Cold War, and a subsequent review of the role of the Pentagon. These events raise issues directly related to the discussion on competitiveness. Moreover, the persistence of national economic problems arising at least in part from the continued poor performance of U.S. industry has refocused attention on competitiveness policy. Three themes pervade the reorientation of competitiveness policy under the Bush administration: rethinking the Pentagon's role, targeting critical technologies for development, and presidential reluctance in the face of a Congress seemingly determined to enact a technology policy.

The Pentagon has long been a major supporter of R&D. Primarily through the Defense Advanced Research Project Agency (DARPA), DOD has been able to channel R&D funds to industry without the red tape so common in other government agencies. Before it was popular, DARPA followed the policy that the best defense for the country lay not only in funding weapons but in providing money for commercial technologies. In the 1960s and 1970s, DARPA's investment in computer research had an enormous impact on the country. But with the end of the Cold War and subsequent peace dividend discussions, DARPA's funding base was targeted for cuts. Demands for the creation of a civilian-DARPA have come from Congress (especially Senator Albert Gore, Jr. of Tennessee). The administration resisted such demands in 1989 and even sent up trial balloons to Congress to see if budget cuts for DARPA and Sematech would be tolerated (Markoff 1989). Congress, however, has not allowed the president his cuts. In the 1991 budget, DARPA's budget is up 16.7 percent from 1990 and Sematech's has remained unchanged (Hamilton 1990).

Sematech has moved to increase the role of DOD in funding civilian R&D. Pressing economic distress in the computer industry has forced Sematech to expand its role from that of R&D consortium coordinator to financing the businesses that are developing the new computer chips. Sematech insists it needs more government funding to accomplish its mission—providing the U.S. semiconductor industry with R&D assistance so that domestically designed and manufactured chips will be competitive with Japanese chips by 1993 (Hayes 1990).

The Pentagon's role is also being rethought in terms of Cold War and post-Persian Gulf War restrictions on international trade. Easing of export controls on technology for what was the Soviet Union and Eastern Europe while more carefully reviewing exports to unstable Third World countries is the recommendation coming from the National Academy of Sciences (Lachica 1991). Indeed, the United States and its allies had voted in 1990 to loosen the trade restrictions on many items covered by the Coordiating Committee for Multilateral Export Controls (CoCom) (Marshall 1991a).

Two competitive issues are central here. First, the demand of the markets of the former Soviet Union republics and Eastern Europe for computers and other technology could significantly improve the U.S. competitive position, especially concerning computers. Second, it is apparent that

Iraq's military hardware originated in Europe and the United States (Marshall 1991a). How can trade restrictions be renegotiated so that dangerous technology does not fall into the hands of unscrupulous leaders without putting domestic producers at a disadvantage?

The new role of the Pentagon in domestic competitiveness and a change in the position on targeting technologies can also be seen in the establishment of the Critical Technologies Institute (CTI). This DOD-funded R&D center was established by section 822 of the National Defense Authorization Act for Fiscal Year 1991. CTI is an incorporated, not-for-profit organization that draws its board of trustees from the secretaries, directors (or representatives of) the Office of Science and Technology Policy (OSTP), the Department of Commerce, the Department of Defense, the Department of Energy, the Department of Health and Human Services, the National Aeronautics and Space Administration, the National Science Foundation, the Federal Coordinating Council on Science, Engineering, and Technology, and ten members from selected universities and industries. The mission of CTI is to "identify suitable near-term, mid-term, and long-term national objectives for the research, development, and production capability of the United States" with respect to critical technologies and to "prepare possible strategies for achieving the identified objectives, including a discussion of the appropriate roles of industry, colleges and universities, and Federal and State agencies."

How does this U.S. MITI identify critical technologies? The White House's Critical Technology Panel issued a report. The Bush administration, resistive yet finally bowing to Congress, agreed to this provision in the National Defense Authorization Act. William D. Phillips, chair of the National Critical Technologies Panel and associate director of OSTP, acknowledged the recent congressional rationalization for both the Critical Technologies Panel and CTI by saying: "We most recently have been reminded, by the spectacular performance of U.S. coalition forces in the Persian Gulf, of the crucial role that technology plays in military competitiveness. It is equally clear that technology plays a similar role in the economic competitiveness among nations" (Tolchin 1991).

Indeed, after the Persian Gulf War, many in Congress were voicing the sentiment that if the country were willing to invest as much in commercial technologies as we do in Patriot missiles, perhaps the United States could regain some of its lost competitiveness. The Senate majority leader, George Mitchell, echoed the general frustration by saying: "If we can make the best smart bomb, can't we make the best VCR?" (Pollack 1991). The patience of Congress to tolerate second-rate industrial performance while continuing to pour huge sums into military R&D seems limited. This is especially the case when many consider the weapons under development far too exotic to have spin-offs for commercialization.

In April 1991, the Critical Technologies Panel identified 22 critical technologies. This was the first time the White House had attempted to prioritize the technologies the country should pursue. The commitment of the administration to lead, however, is untested. The Bush administration has demonstrated a reluctance to intervene in market processes and may not provide the strength of leadership Congress believes is necessary. Mere identification of critical technologies will do little if presidential support is not forthcoming. Nonetheless, for some observers such a move signals a real change in the White House.

There are other indications of a shifting posture as well. In February 1990, for instance, President Bush also created the long-awaited President's Council of Advisors on Science and Technology. This council, akin to the Council of Economic Advisors, raises S&T advice to the highest level of government since the Kennedy administration. Bush had promised to create the advisory group during the presidential campaign but it remains to be seen what real policy influence the 13 scientists and engineers will have (Dowd 1990).

In another instance of moderating executive attitude, after two years of congressional agitation, the Commerce Department has been given funding for five regional centers for technology development (Marshall 1991b). These centers are nonprofit industrial research centers that use taxpayer dollars to directly develop generic commercial technologies.

Perhaps the most telling indication of a shift in the White House is the existence of a document entitled "U.S. Technology Policy" released by the Bush administration in November 1990 (Marshall 1991b). While this publication may be thin on specifics, it provides justification for federal government agency funding of industrial technologies that have no direct national security link. This indicates a modification of the last ten years of established policy directions.

CONCLUSION

Whether it is called by the name "competitiveness," "technology", or "industrial" policy, a new area of government activity has emerged over the past ten years. At the outset competitiveness policy was restricted by a conservative ideology in which industry support not associated with basic research or military development was anathema. Support for basic research had been long accepted as an appropriate role for government, while national defense concerns were rarely questioned. Under this umbrella, competitiveness policy took root during the Reagan administration. Reagan-era competitive policy was focused on three basics: reduction of antitrust prosecution, increasing technology transfer, and precompetitive R&D cooperation.

Moderation of competitiveness policy is beginning to occur. Freely using the name "technology policy," the old ideological restrictions seem to be fading as a consequence of continued economic distress and mounting congressional aggressiveness. The need to justify federal expenditure on technological development in narrow military terms is easing. National security has taken on a new meaning and part of this new meaning is economic success in a technologically competitive world. As a consequence, programs and policies are moderating. Outright assistance to industry is no longer looked at askance. The notion of strategic national planning for a healthy and competitive private sector is being reconsidered. In the process of selecting the right technologies to back, scientific and engineering advice is being solicited at the highest level of government. And the insistence of Congress that—willing or not—the executive must lead seems unrelenting.

REFERENCES

Bayh-Dole Act of 1980, PL 96–517, enacted December 12, 1980.

Dowd, Maureen. 1990. Bush appoints 13 to science panel. *New York Times* 3 February, 1A.

Ewing, Ky P. 1980. Joint research projects and antitrust. *Chemical and Engineering News* 58 (9): 5.

————. 1981. Joint research, antitrust, and innovation. *Research Management* 24 (2): 25–29.

Federal Technology Transfer Act of 1986, PL 99–502, enacted October 20, 1986.

Finegan, Jay. 1987. Uncle Sam, research director. *Inc.* 9 (2): 23–26.

Gannes, Stuart. 1988. The good news about U.S. r&d. *Fortune* 117 (3): 48–56.

Glassie, Jefferson C. 1987. Heading off antitrust with smart research. *Association Management* 39 (4): 61–63.

Guterl, Fred. 1987. Technology transfer isn't working. *Business Month* 130 (3): 44–48.

Hamilton, David P. 1990. Technology policy: Congress takes the reins. *Science* 250 (4982): 747.

Hayes, Thomas C. 1990. Sematech today: Cash dispenser. *New York Times* 4 January, 1D.

Krieger, James H. 1987. Cooperation key to U.S. technology remaining competitive. *Chemical Engineering News* 65 (17): 24–26.

Lachica, Eduardo. 1991. Panel urges easing technology curbs on Soviet Union. *Wall Street Journal* 1 February, 4B.

Lambright, W. Henry and Dianne Rahm. 1991. Science, technology and the states. *Forum for Applied Research and Public Policy* 6 (3): 49–60.

Markoff, John. 1989. Re-evaluation is urged on cutting high-tech aid. *New York Times* 11 November, 2D.

Marshall, Eliot. 1991a. War with Iraq spurs new export controls. *Science* 251 (4993): 512–514.

———. 1991b. U.S. technology strategy emerges. *Science* 252 (5002): 20–24.

Murray, Thomas J. 1981. R&D tax shelters are catching on. *Dun's Business Month* 118 (6): 86–87.

National Competitiveness Technology Transfer Act of 1989, PL 101–189, section 3131, enacted November 29, 1989.

National Cooperative Research Act of 1984, PL 98–462, enacted October 11, 1984.

National Defense Authorization Act for Fiscal Years 1990 and 1991, PL 101–189, enacted November 29, 1989.

National Defense Authorization Act for Fiscal Year 1991, PL 101–510, enacted November 5, 1990.

Norris, William C. 1983. R&d cooperation must be fostered. *Electronics* 55 (6): 24.

Omnibus Trade and Competitiveness Act of 1988, PL 100–418, enacted August 23, 1988.

Palca, Joseph. 1990. NSF: Hard times amid plenty. *Science* 248 (4955): 541–543.

Pollack, Andrew. 1991. In U.S. technology, a gap between arms and VCR's. *New York Times* 4 March, 1A.

Rahm, Dianne, Barry Bozeman, and Michael Crow. 1988. Technology transfer and competitiveness: An empirical assessment of the roles of university and government research and development labs. *Public Administration Review* 48 (6): 969–978.

Rahm, Dianne and Thomas F. Luce, Jr. 1992. Issues in the design of state science- and technology-based economic development programs: The case of Pennsylvania's Ben Franklin partnership. *Economic Development Quarterly* 6(1): 41–51.

Reagan, Ronald. 1984. Executive Order 12428—President's Commission on Industrial Competitiveness, June 28, 1983. *Public Papers of the Presidents of the United States*, Book 1, January 1—July 1, 1983. Washington, DC: U.S. Government Printing Office.

Small Business Innovation Development Act of 1982, PL 97–219, enacted July 22, 1982.

Stevenson-Wydler Technology Innovation Act of 1980, PL 96–480, enacted October 21, 1980.

Technology Competitiveness Act. See House Report 100–266 (August 4, 1987) and Senate Report 100–80 (June 22, 1987) and Title V, Subtitle B of the

Omnibus Trade and Competitiveness Act of 1988, PL 100–418, enacted August 23, 1988.

Tolchin, Martin. 1990. Antitrust limit voted by house. *New York Times* 6 June, 1D.

————. 1991. White House lists 22 critical technologies. *New York Times* 26 April, 17D.

Trademark Clarification Act of 1984, PL 98–620, enacted November 8, 1984.

U.S. Congress. Congressional Budget Office. 1988. *Using federal r&d to promote commercial innovation.* Washington, DC: U.S. Government Printing Office.

Zwart, Sara G. 1987. The new antitrust: An aerial view of joint ventures and mergers. *Journal of Business Strategy* 7 (Spring): 68–76.

2 Decontrolling Technology Transfer for American Competitiveness

Brack Brown

COMPETITION CONTROVERSY: DUEL OVER DUAL-USE TECHNOLOGIES

Enhanced economic competitiveness has been closely linked in the U.S. national debate on the subject with the need to increase the variety, quality, and marketing of new technologies. Some of the suggestions for accomplishing these objectives through public means have been to tighten the ground rules affecting international trade, such as patent enforcement, increasing resources for science education, equalizing tariffs, liberalizing antitrust rules, providing more federal (R&D) incentives, and offering new tax credits. There has also been an avalanche of recommendations offering ways to enhance creativity, efficiency, better commercial utilization of federal research, and export incentives. A steadily increasing number of articles, books, and government reports have been written on how to accomplish these objectives.

The question posed in this chapter is what is the bearing on competitiveness of government efforts to stimulate the development and transfer of new technologies here and abroad while impeding their acquisition by adversaries whose use of them might impair U.S. national security? To answer the question we will be alternately discussing various aspects of technology transfer process and the U.S. technology transfer control system and policy.

The passing of the Stevenson-Wydler Technology Innovation Act of 1980 appeared to put government in the forefront of moving new research toward early applications in domestic and international markets. The plan was to have every relevant federal agency (defense labs initially excluded) use its facilities and talents to expedite links between advanced research activity, on the one hand and applications in the economy and among state and local governments, on the other. When the act was passed, supporters saw it as a powerful vehicle for stimulating productive domestic technology transfer. Within a few years concerns grew about the U.S. eroding competitive position, especially in several technologies in which it had long been world leader. That trend has continued to the present day.

The competitive posture of the United States has also been affected by other government efforts, ones that intensified over the last decade, to prevent or inhibit the flow of "certain" critical technologies to U.S. adversaries. This was done principally through extension and enforcement of the Export Act of 1979 and its many amendments. Export controls over trade with adversarial countries can be traced back to the Trading With the Enemy Act of 1917 and the Neutrality Act of 1935. The basic features of the current system were set up in the Export Control Act of 1949, the same year NATO was established (Wallerstein with Snyder in National Academy of Sciences 1991).

Export controls came to include a strong domestic technology licensing and an international enforcement regime to enable the United States and its allies to prevent, intercept, or delay the transfer of technologically valuable knowledge or its experimental or commercial applications to countries that might use the technology to gain some *military* advantage over the United States.

In many ways enhancing economic competitiveness through government policies to stimulate innovation and trade has been at odds with efforts to meet national security concerns by preventing many specific technologies from being readily transferred across national boundaries. Policies to stimulate national technological development and trade have in practice not coexisted well with restraints on sharing technical information and denying export licenses to business selling certain products overseas.

TERMS OF DISCOURSE: MEANINGS OF TECHNOLOGY TRANSFER

Efforts to understand and to enhance technological diffusion and transfer for productive human purposes go back many years. Transfer of anything is conceptually a particular case of a cultural activity called diffusion. Diffusion refers to the spreading by any means of a new idea, thing, or practice from a source to subsequent users. Transfer, however, is a spreading out to a new user or users who are aware of and attempt to model theirs on the experience of the donor(s). This may apply to fads or chemical formulas. Transfer therefore is a relatively conscious and deliberate act (Rogers 1983; Furash 1971).

It would be helpful in studying issues related to the transfer of technology to have more consistency in the use of terms than we now have. Assessing and comparing findings from diverse fields of research and in different settings, from the factory floor to relations between nations, poses endless problems of determining what are the parallel concepts and patterns. Lacking this, it is hard to deduce general principles of diffusion, innovation, and transfer from the evidence when authorities differ so widely on terminology and meaning. This confusing situation has often been noted in the literature (Downs and Mohr 1967). The variety of meanings can be so confusing that some authors will refuse to use a term like transfer to avoid the problem (Twiss 1986).

There are many examples of misuse or oversimplification of this terminology. The simple division of domestic and international technology transfer, for example, is a very crude dichotomy. People who use this division seldom address the U.S. need to acquire technology from other countries. The term "managing innovation" often confuses invention with innovation or equates innovation with minor improvements that are neither novel nor substantial. Inventing is an original, one-time creative act, while the application of invention is innovation, even if done by the inventor. To complicate things, innovation is often treated as a buzz word—a loose synonym for improvement, trying something different, or simply change.

Technology transfer clearly has many different meanings but there is an unfortunate tendency by many writers to act as though their meaning is universally understood and accepted. They may employ the term to refer to the transfer of research findings into useful commercial products, but it may also refer to applications of research to new processes and structures. Another meaning of transfer is the adoption of recently developed innovations to unprecedented uses or simply to uses new in particular industrial, governmental, military, or other settings. It can also refer to international technical assistance activities in which more affluent donor countries assist poorer recipient countries in adopting *any* technologies, whether innovative or not, that promise to enable the poorer country to achieve its material or policy goals. Finally, transfer can refer to the efforts of *any* country, technologically developed or not, to borrow (or buy) what it considers useful knowledge or practices from any other country beyond its borders. The United States, for reasons discussed later, often fails to see the inherent benefits of fostering two-way transfers.

One of the fundamental starting points for understanding any aspect of technology transfer is that it is an absolutely natural and ubiquitous process in human activity (Barnett 1953). It partly explains such things as how fire making (mythical and actual) came to be used throughout the world. Recognizing the universality of the process helps us to understand also that enhancing competitiveness is only one of a host of objectives that technology transfer may address. In fact, improving the kinds and qualities of U.S. industrial goods to make them more attractive exportables is only *one* dimension of competitiveness. So the relationship between competitiveness and technology transfer is extremely complicated and invites much more basic research than has so far been done.

Many researchers engaged in technological innovation and transfer studies appear to be only dimly aware of the social science scholarship on the subject over the past half century (Barnett 1953; Havelock 1969; Rogers and Shoemaker 1971; as well as numerous studies contracted by the National Science Foundation, the Department of Housing and Urban Development, the National Institutes of Mental Health, and other agencies). Government policy advisors and policymakers have also often failed to utilize available knowledge about these subjects. This observation motivated those who established the journal *Knowledge Utilization* and the *Technology Transfer Journal*. In these journals technology transfer controls is a minor theme, but ways of promoting useful transfers of all kinds are well covered.

With respect to competition, three kinds of transfer phenomena stand out. Each can and does interact with the other. The first is the transfer of research results (from federal labs, industry, or universities) to technical applications. This involves the link between invention or discovery (original ideas) and innovation. Innovation, as Dennis Gabor (1970, 1) defines it, is "all novelties that once created can be usefully and repeatedly applied." Government concerns about ways to stimulate the generation of new technologies led to the passage of the Stevenson-Wydler Act in 1980.

The second type of transfer deals with the conversion of innovative technologies (not inventions, but early applications) into commercially viable items, widely attractive to the market. Hardware products are but one manifestation of such technology. New materials, computer programs, or ways of transmitting messages might be the innovations. Turning them into competitive items involves identifying, supporting, and then disseminating them to industry or other users—in other words, accelerating their introduction in the economy.

The third type of transfer is the one that impacts most directly on export competition; it is the transfer of technologies through licensed sales, franchises, coproduction, or other arrangements into the markets of the world. The movement of new technologies from one country to another, by any deliberate means, is what we mean by international technology transfer. But by its nature it is a two-way street. Every nation may seek something new from another nation and attempt to extract a trade advantage in that item, if it can.

Each of the three aspects of transfer has its own set of special conditions and objectives. Each is but a subsystem of a larger system of technology diffusion. Until the era of technology controls, the primary scholarly concern with all these levels was how to understand, harness, and enhance them for productive use by anybody. The *promotion* of technology transfer in all forms was believed to be a key to greater human productivity and advancement. It still is.

RISE OF SECURITY CONTROLS: PERCEIVED PERILS

In 1949 the United States established the Coordinating Committee for Multilateral Export Controls (CoCom) to limit the amount of military technology acquired by communist nations. Little technology that was produced in the civil sector that had both military and commercial applications was included. But by the late '70s and early '80s the Defense Department was convinced that government should restrict dual-use technologies and get CoCom members to do the same. Long lists of critical technologies were prepared. Force was added to the argument by the publication of a Defense Science Board task force report on dual-use technologies, which greatly influenced the adoption of the Export Administration Act of 1979 in its provision for denying the Soviet military *and* industrial base of useful technologies (U.S. Department of Defense 1976). A detailed analysis of later events, including the establishment of a new DOD agency, The Defense Technology Security Administration, is analyzed in a recent article by Sherry Rice (1990).

In support of the tightening of technology controls, especially in licensing of firms selling dual-use items, the Pentagon and the Central Intelligence Agency (CIA) released reports about illegal transfers and dramatic interceptions of controlled national security technologies. Cases of diversion included very high speed integrated circuits, sonar devices, nuclear triggers, and long-range cannon tubing. The most celebrated case of the high stakes of failing to control technology was provided by the illegal acquisition by the former Soviet Union of silent propeller technology to make their submarines less detectable.

The Reagan administration in its first several years conducted a full-court press to beef up controls. In an early 1984 Defense Department report to Congress, Defense Secretary Weinberger opened his remarks on DOD's technology transfer control program—later, technology transfer security program—with these words:

I am pleased to report to the Congress that the Department of Defense is fulfilling your mandate to protect America's key technologies and military systems. In its first thousand days, the Reagan Administration has reversed the tide of a decade of neglect and naivete and has made technology transfer control a key element of national security policy (U.S. Department of Defense 1984).

The preface to a widely distributed CIA white paper more than a year later underlined the perceived threat as follows:

In recent years, the U.S. Government has learned of a massive, well-organized campaign by the Soviet Union to acquire Western technology illegally and legally for its weapons and military equipment projects. Each year Moscow receives thousands of pieces of Western equipment and many tens of thousands of unclassified, classified, and proprietary documents as part of this campaign. The assimilation of Western technology is so broad that the U.S. and other Western nations are thus subsidizing the Soviet military buildup (U.S. CIA 1985).

THE COSTS OF TECHNOLOGY CONTROLS

Although advocates of control said there was not much new about technology control efforts, there have been a dramatic expansion, stricter enforcement, many new rules, new units created, and higher level political emphasis and involvement. Control measures in the eyes of some opponents violated traditions of U.S. openness. They have been only spottily enforced. They reduced the capacity of U.S. businesses to respond to market opportunities. They provoked unnecessary rivalry among enforcement agencies (DOD, Commerce, Customs, and the State Department), created serious tensions with our trading and business partners overseas, and encouraged pervasive evasion strategies on the part of U.S. and foreign firms. Allan Shinn, Jr. (1990) has even argued that controls may violate constitutional principles through prior restraint and by being overbroad.

Arm twisting of allies and trading partners to conform their technology control activities to those desired by the United States made many of them resentful of the U.S. insistence on the extraterritorial reach of their laws. According to a special science panel report, *Finding Common Ground: U.S. Export Controls in a Changed Global Environment*, this has encouraged CoCom nations to ignore or make many exceptions to the informal screening activities they were set up to perform (National Academy of Sciences 1991).

The question of the relative costs and benefits of tight controls versus more open trade has also taken a toll in domestic agency rivalry. Rice (1990, 220) writes that "the Reagan administration divided itself into bellicose feuding departments and serious worry infects the Commission of the European Community."

Imposing restrictions on the outflow of technology may also have affected U.S. industrial incentives to innovate. Excessive measures to control scientific information, including the ill-fated FBI effort to monitor public library use by people with foreign names, engendered disrespect in the scientific community. Both our Japanese and European partners on NASA's international space station were frustrated by U.S. efforts to control access to certain technical systems on the station. Frustrating the progress of other nations, especially partners, by denying them fair access to the latest technical advances is considered a spoiling strategy, not a competitive strategy, and one that could cut both ways.

It remains an empirical rather than an ideological question whether the ratio of gains in security compared to those lost in competitiveness mattered. One argument that may have been valid was that an aggressive policy of technology denial made the Soviets more convinced of the need for accepting new strategic and conventional arms agreements. But it is not certain whether these pressures or the unsustainable economic path of the Soviets had more to do with their dramatic economic and arms treaty reforms in the late '80s.

Though DOD has been required to take part in and *encourage* the development and domestic transfer of competitive technologies, its main concerns remained with control, a position that enjoyed strong backing from the White House. While President Reagan characterized the Soviets as the "Evil Empire" in the early '80s, in only a few years' time the Soviet regime was appearing to be more like the kingdom of Oz. The likelihood that a few years of strengthened dual-use export controls accounted for much of this change is doubtful. This is not to suggest that continuing and improved controls over the transfer of military technologies per se did not make a large difference.

It is, however, problematical whether *any* of all the reported diversions and illegal sales of dual-use items would have made any significant difference in America's overall security posture. While many advocates of the primacy of security tried to make the virtue of denying technology to our adversaries a necessity, business and economic writers tried to make the necessity of compliance with export restrictions and technology security rules more of a virtue than it probably was. Neither the civilian nor the military side responded very quickly to the sea changes in world markets, world politics, and world technology.

It was not until the release of the Allen Report *Balancing the National Interest*, that it become clear controls had imposed measurable economic costs for American technology and trade (National Academy of Sciences 1987). The Allen Report substantially affected the passage of the Omnibus Trade Act of 1988, in which the scales tipped back in favor of Commerce's position on liberalized controls. However, the act also supported stiffer penalties for those who violated transfer rules—especially because the technology control lists were to be considerably shortened.

The United States may be the first democratic country to have erected elaborate control barriers to the *outflow* of technology. The approach not only ignores the cultural dynamics of technological diffusion, it is also ideologically out of synchrony with U.S. beliefs in free trade, the free circulation of scientific findings, and open competition.

COMPETITION: TECHNOLOGY ON A CHANGING GLOBE

Changed National Economic Interests

The idea that security controls can be imposed on the research activity and products of "American" firms is challenged in an economic argument put forward by Robert Reich (1990–91) in an article, "Does Corporate Nationality Matter?" He argues that U.S. competitiveness policy should be based on company behavior, not ownership. Reich says "more than 20 percent of the output of U.S. firms is now produced by foreign workers on foreign soil, and the percentage is rising quickly" (p. 41). In addition, U.S. firms spent 30 percent more on overseas R&D between 1986 and 1988, a faster growth than domestic R&D investments. Thus a strictly national calculation of benefits can be misleading.

In this latter notion is a presumption that there is a distinctly U.S. technology and a distinctly U.S. set of industrial interests that can be protected by controls. Leaving aside the whole issue of multinational corporations, corporate nationality itself is perhaps becoming passé as a basis for identifying the source of a technology. To Reich, "the logic of global capitalism, in fact, requires that U.S. firms allocate their production across many nations, wherever they can earn the highest return for their shareholders" (p. 42). He goes so far as to say that "even when it comes to national security, the fact of U.S. corporate nationality is less relevant than the location of product" (p. 42.). Laws and policies designed to stem the tide of declining competitiveness are incorrectly premised on the notion that "the competitiveness of the U.S. corporation is roughly equivalent to the competitiveness of the United States" (p. 42).

The fuzziness and uncertainty about the role of national interest is of growing concern, and arguments for revised interpretations are appearing (Tonelson 1991). Support for a more classical view comes from Thomas Murrin (1990), deputy secretary of the Department of Commerce, who notes:

It is well and good to talk about the benefits of internationalization, but if our country wishes to ensure both its economic and military security, we have no choice but to make our own national interest top priority—even as we work towards greater sharing of new technologies that can be put to work for the common good.

To Murrin, an "America first" policy toward competitor nations would limit foreigners owning U.S. plants while they keep their know-how at home; resist foreign investment in U.S. universities, which gives the competitors initial access, perhaps even control over research results; and strictly enforce trade laws to prevent dumping and export price subsidizations. Not only is the concept of national economic interests undergoing great scrutiny, so is the idea of security interests.

Changed Security Interests

In the past few years the thick veil of secrecy surrounding former Soviet and East Bloc security and security arrangements has been badly torn. At the same time the West has vastly increased its capacity to monitor their activities. This combination of factors alone puts the United States in a tremendously advantaged security position. Space-based surveillance and eavesdropping along with greater openness and exchange have tipped the balance in the U.S. direction so dramatically that the question of the cost-effectiveness of present controls over technology transfer has had to be raised. And as Western security is subjected to less threat, broad openings to new market opportunities in the East vastly increase the competitive opportunities for U.S. businesses to penetrate new high technology markets and participate in the formation of whole new economies in Eastern Europe.

The Soviet president himself personally pleaded with the Group of Seven leaders "to help the Soviet Union join the world free-market system and rescue the country from economic disaster" (*Washington Post* 1991, 1). On the same day the U.S. and Soviet presidents "reached final agreement on the first treaty of the atomic age to actually reduce [by one third] their arsenals of long-range nuclear weapons."

Under these changed conditions, an increasing favorable climate exists for letting the incentives of openness of information and markets operate under a more tailored and simplified control regime. This would not mean ignoring international situations in which an absence of control might strongly contribute to regional or East-West military imbalance. However, it must be repeated that in the period following East Bloc reform and the Gulf War there is a huge de facto security imbalance in favor of the United States.

Changed Global Technology

According to Homer Barnett, (1953), in a foundation study of innovation, it is easy to track a great number of very significant innovations over the whole course of human history. In his view, new productive tools emerge from the worldwide culture, not from a single society. It is worldwide diffusion that determines the extent to which ideas will be exchanged. At the same time we will find some cultures that have tried to isolate their people from or resist the introduction of outside technology. But in the contemporary world it is more common for cultures to utilize new technologies no matter from where they come. Today the variety of sources of high technology products and know-how has increased opportunities and stimulated demand so much that it is improbable that any one nation by itself can make a difference in what is available to any other nation. One article on export controls notes in this regard, "information technologies have in the past decade become more powerful, more diverse, more plentiful, more dispersed, and more affordable than almost any observer might have imagined. The implications for export controls are significant" (Goodman et al. 1989–90, 59).

Architects of the export control system have discovered that there are many points at which transfer could be interrupted and have concentrated on many of these choke points. However, it is a major point of this discussion that trying to block any channel of technology's flow is like trying to prevent a dike from overflowing by putting one's finger in a leaking hole. The inclinations of creators, sellers, and buyers of technology will usually be to find ways to overcome bureaucratic efforts to dam up the technology. Being one of those riding on the bow wave of technology development is probably a better way to exploit new technology than expending great energies to contain it.

The United States is increasingly being displaced as the sole or major provider of many kinds of knowledge or technology sought by other countries. The availability of new science and technology from non-U.S. sources has increased manyfold, as Goodman notes above. With so many wide new avenues for scientific, technical, and economic cooperation and a changed global security situation, we have only started on the path to a comprehensive review of export controls and transfer policies (Bertsch et al. 1991).

CONNECTED ENVIRONMENTS: COMPETITION AS COOPERATION

The inability of single entities to control outcomes in certain kinds of environments was noted in the literature several decades ago by Emery and Trist (1978). They characterized the kinds of environments with increasing connectedness as type IV, or textured environments.

Continuing technological change in particular is an ubiquitous process whose impact has now altered the world environment at all levels of organization. Emery and Trist, grappling with the implications of the changes, extended systems theory to address exchanges *between* organizations within variable kinds of environments. They held that what was missing was a consideration of "those processes in the environment itself which are among the determining conditions of exchanges," which they dubbed the "causal texture" or patterned connectedness of the environment (p. 217). Environments themselves have become organized, some to the point where they are no longer a direct function of what an organization does or any of its immediate relationships.

The American and CoCom export control systems were developed atheoretically—that is, without relationship to any particular theoretical models of innovation, diffusion, transfer, or systems (Roiter 1990). Yet during the '80s, when new controls were being developed, a profound change was taking place in the texture of the international technical environment. The technology generation and transfer systems of various countries and regions were becoming complexly and intricately connected with each other in ways resembling Emery and Trist's ideal type IV environment.

Emery and Trist describe their third ideal type environment as follows: It "consists of a clustered environment in which there is more than one system of the same kind, i.e., the objects of one organization are the same as, or relevant to [specific] others like it. Competitors seek to improve their own chances by hindering each other" (p. 221). This was the implicit view of the environment held by the late Carter and early Reagan administrations and one consistent with the model of power politics.

Emery and Trist go on to say that "unlike type III, in the fourth type, or turbulent field environment, the dynamic properties [of organizational relations] do not arise simply from the interaction of the component organizations, but from the field itself. The 'ground' is in motion" (p. 221). Important consequences flow from this. First, there is much more uncertainty; second, direct action to achieve one entity's objectives becomes more risky; third, zero-sum-type competitive strategies become less reliable; and fourth (and most important), interdependence and cooperative strategies optimize adaptability for all parties. This is closer to the de facto new world order that has taken shape in recent years.

The optimum policy, under the type IV conditions just described is to pursue agreement on new mutual values, establishing a matrix of organizations that offers "the maximum convergence as regards the interests of *other* parties" (p. 221, emphasis added). In other words, cooperative strategies reduce turbulence in such environments better than can competition. In contemporary terms, this is a prescription for collaborative security and trade relationships as well as a strategy of conflict resolution rather than power politics.

These new perspectives may be what we have been seeing in many recent U.S. policy recommendations affecting industrial, sectoral, public-private, and international interactions: a call for collaboration and partnership, a new set of values. The new prescription, especially in regard to export regulations, has even been interpreted in the latest major report on trade and export control policy to mean that the United States should have as among its primary objectives *support* for economic and political reform in the former Soviet Union and Eastern Europe (National Academy of Sciences 1991).

THWARTED INNOVATION PROMOTION POLICY

The tension between controlling technology transfers and facilitating it has nowhere been more evident than in steps to make federal labs (more than 200 of them) more aware of the linkages between federal R&D and the commercial utilization of new technologies. Institutionalizing involvement of the labs was a major objective of the 1985 amendments to the Stevenson-Wydler Act of 1980. In testimony to Congress, Dr. Bruce

Merrifield, assistant secretary in the Department of Commerce, described the various ways the transfer of federally funded technology to the private sector was being pursued through the 1980 act: "That Law was designed to stimulate productivity, technology, and innovation in the private sector for the purpose of regaining or maintaining U.S. technology and industry leadership in global markets" (U.S. Congress, House 1985, 22). Merrifield noted that worldwide technological development meant that the United States had to accelerate its technology productivity efforts. "It's a globally competitive situation, and the need is to remove the barriers now to the transfer of technology and to provide more incentives to make that happen more expeditiously" (p. 26).

The gist of most of the testimony on extending Stevenson-Wydler was that technology transfer, with strong support from top leadership, should be made an assigned duty of all government labs. Belief in the need for official measures to facilitate transfer to U.S. companies was nearly unanimous and the shadow of control was seldom mentioned. Senator Donald Riegle at the outset of one of the hearings noted: "Today's hearing focuses specifically on the Stevenson Wydler Innovation Act of 1980. Stevenson Wydler is the one program enacted over the past 5 years that addresses the problem. Yet the administration has virtually ignored the program" (U.S. Congress, Senate 1985, 2 *[New Technologies on Economic Competitiveness]*).

Only two clear acknowledgements of control barriers were mentioned at the hearings. One, paradoxically, came from General Richard Thompson, U.S. Army, who said:

We should make it abundantly clear that domestic technology transfer is as potentially beneficial to the public as [is] new product R&D. . . . We would also recommend that those responsible for limiting the release of technology (export control) have a very close working relationship with those responsible for domestic technology transfer to assure that the right hand knows what the left hand is doing and why (p. 21).

The other remark in the same series of hearings was made by Lionel Olmer, undersecretary for trade in the Department of Commerce. Olmer, responding to a question about his views of the recommendations of the President's Commission on Industrial Competitiveness, said:

Now, whether or not the [recommended amendments to] the [Export Administration] act are going to minimize the impact of controls on competitiveness is a subjective judgement to make. It is going to have an impact on competitiveness and there is no way it can't. Its intent is to prevent the diversion of high technology flowing to our adversaries. And that represents a cost (p. 90).

Federal laboratory facilities have had to contend with at least two contradictory mandates: first, to think more commercially in order to put public R&D dollars in the service of a more competitive America; and second, to observe both proprietal and security restraints intended to limit dissemination of information about innovations. Their response was biased toward increasing protection until about 1985; then the pendulum swung away from that position. But in the labs and agencies, designated technology transfer officers often barely understood their roles or they defined them very narrowly. Many officials at the lab or bureau level were oblivious that there is even a tension between technology transfer facilitation and control because the attention and resources on behalf of control made it a clear priority.

Many of the critical transfer-promoting institutions and bureaus established by the president and Congress, backed by coordinating councils on trade and competitiveness and task and interagency groups, were seldom given the funds, mandates, or staff to be fully effective. Among the organizations created were the Federal Laboratory Consortium, various agency "excellence centers," technology information clearinghouses, and units of the National Science Foundation. Programs for the promotion of innovation and transfer remain underdeveloped, uncoordinated, and underutilized though long advocated by consultants, legislators, professional groups, and many within the administration itself.

For more than a decade the debates and decisions about trade policy, science and technology policy, and industrial policy have been dominated by an ideological preoccupation with three initiatives: first, eliminating government interventions in the economy; second, raising commercial consciousness in the agencies; and third, protecting our military lead in critical technology on the international front. Meanwhile many of the important linkages between science, technology, innovation, technology transfer, and changes in the global technology environment were not fully appreciated nor integrated in government policy. In the struggle between technology transfer facilitation and control, facilitation for many years has been a clear loser.

COMPETITIVE SECURITY CONTROLS

The issue now causing splits in our own government, between it and the business and scientific communities, and in the Western alliance, is the desirable balance point between technology protection and openness (National Academy of Sciences 1991). On the one hand, there are few objections to operating an export control system that prevents advanced Western technology reaching those who might use it for military or terrorist purposes against our security interests. On the other hand, the United States cannot afford self-imposed obstacles to the health of its industrial-technology base or to its trade improvement agenda. But there remains great confusion about achieving that balance. Rice (1990, 233) concludes:

Research on the difficult question of which high technology goods and when to export [them] to the Soviet bloc reflects the significant forces currently reshaping policy. The rise of Mikhail Gorbachev, the decline of Western defense budgets, the prospects of an integrated common European market, and basic changes in the international political economy have cast serious doubt on the assumptions that the technology export management concepts and institutions of the postwar era can or should survive into the 1990's. . . . [T]he research reflects a growing descensus among students of the subject and in too many instances, an absence of agreement about the facts to say nothing of their policy implications.

The National Academy Study, *Finding Common Ground* (1991, 182) probably best represents the new thinking about how to address security concerns while minimizing trade interference in dual-use technologies. It calls for the stringent prioritizing of export control categories and lists; robust enforcement of means for protecting technology that have clear military significance; a major reorientation of controls to deal with proliferation of the weapons of mass destruction and advanced conventional weapons making them a more explicit national and multilateral security concern; and a much more effective dispute resolution arrangement among the coordinating agencies. Specifically the study called for "progressive removal of export controls on dual use items to the Soviet Union and the East European countries for commercial end uses that can be verified."

TRANSFORMATIONAL TECHNOLOGY TRANSFER POLICY

A much freer flow of innovations, given the increasing number of nations capable of creating important technological improvements, would improve our scientific vitality, technical leadership, and market position. The control mentality has long interfered with research aimed at fostering inventiveness, transfer of innovation, and creative trade responses to a changing global environment.

If the resources of the U.S. government devoted to controlling technology over the last decade had been invested in research, methods, and institutions to *stimulate* innovation and technology transfer, such as fully backing and funding the Stevenson-Wydler Act and its 1985 amendments, the U.S. technological and competitive position might be far stronger than it is. Many earlier public program efforts that were meagerly funded or in some cases eliminated contained the seeds of a better approach. Precedents for constructive federal support of technology transfer promotion have been chronicled in works by Hough (1977), Doctors (1976), and the National Science Foundation (Tornatsky et al. 1983).

It is not too late to overcome the self-defeating behavior we have engaged in for so many years, though it is possible we may do "too little, too late" to compensate for the steady erosion in our competitive position, which has been so widely noted. The Reagan-Bush administrations have sought to enhance our technological position by eliminating government intervention in domestic technological development and industrial growth in many areas while greatly increasing government intervention in knowledge sharing and trade.

An optimum strategy for directly stimulating U.S. economic competitiveness is to vigorously *encourage* a much higher level of transfer activities at the research, commercialization, and international levels, keeping in mind that international transfer is a two-way process. Active public promotion of technological creation and diffusion exploits an existing U.S. advantage in the size and diversity of its research and industrial base. Riding the bow wave of technology change and being the first to *share* it through cooperative projects is a desirable strategy. We must avoid losing from economic protectionism what we seem to be gaining from a reformed control regime and a safer global environment.

Rice (1990) thought there was cause to worry on this score. Noting that it was the Department of Commerce (DOC) that had shot down a cooperative initiative with the Japanese to build the FSX fighter, she observed: "This new protectionist stance by the DOC may signal a new era in promoting U.S. competition by sheltering U.S. technological leads rather than encouraging international trade." If this is true we could compound the mistakes we made earlier with other forms of "protection."

The de facto "new world order" created by the connecting of environments that Emery and Trist talked about demands movement away from a zero-sum, power politics brand of competition. It calls for more investment in conflict prevention and resolution, shared and fairly exchanged basic science and technology, and integration of all states into a fairly based global market.

It also calls for a post-NATO/Warsaw Pact regional security arrangement coupled with disarmament and committed steps toward reducing the proliferation of exotic weapons and weapons of mass destruction. Broadbased, multilateral export controls that support these latter objectives, as well as coping with terrorism, have a meaningful place in future global relationships. Recent steps in renegotiating treaties based on the Conventional Forces in Europe (CFE) and the Conference of Security and Cooperation in Europe (CSCE) would eliminate a great proportion of the threats that enhanced export controls were designed to contain (Sandole 1991). In many regards the reduction of international security threats to all large trading nations should create an environment in which market forces are restrained only by the imagination and energy of innovators, producers, and traders. Decontrol *and* innovation promotion may not only lead to balancing the national interest, but balancing the global interest as well.

REFERENCES

Barnett, Homer. 1953. *Innovation: The basis of cultural change.* New York: McGraw-Hill.

Bertsch, Gary K., Heinrich Vogel, and Jan Zielonka, eds. 1991. *After the revolution: East-West trade and technology transfer.* Boulder, CO: Westview Press.

Doctors, Samuel I. 1969. *The role of federal agencies in technology transfer.* Cambridge, MA: MIT Press.

Downs, George B. and L. B. Mohr. 1967. Conceptual issues in the study of innovation. *Administrative Science Quarterly* 21 (December): 700–714.

Emery, E. F., and E. L. Trist. 1978. The causal texture of organizational environments. In James M. Shafritz and Phillip H. Whitbeck, eds., *Classics of organization theory.* 1965 reprint, Oak Park, IL: Moore.

Furash, Edward E. 1971. The problem of technology transfer. In R. A. Bauer and K. J. Gergen, eds., *The Study of policy formation.* New York: The Free Press.

Gabor, Dennis. 1970. *Innovations: Scientific, technological, and social.* New York: Oxford University Press.

Goodman, Seymour E., Marjory S. Blumenthal, and Gary L. Geipal. 1989–90. Export controls reconsidered. *Issues in Science and Technology* 6 (Winter): 40–44.

Havelock, Ronald. 1969. *Planning for innovation through dissemination and utilization of knowledge.* University of Michigan, Center for the Utilization of Scientific Knowledge.

Hough, Granville W. 1977. *Technology diffusion: Federal programs and procedures.* Mt. Airy, MD: Lomond Books.

Murrin, Thomas J. 1990. Thinking globally, acting nationally. *Issues in Science and Technology* 6 (Summer): 50–54.

National Academy of Sciences. 1987. *Balancing the national interest: U.S. national security export controls and global economic competitiveness* (known as the Allen Report). Washington, DC: National Academy Press.

————. National Academy of Engineering, Institute of Medicine. 1991. *Finding common ground: U.S. export controls in a changed global environment*. Washington, DC: National Academy Press.

Reich, Robert B. 1990–91. Does corporate nationality matter? *Issues in Science and Technology* 6 (Winter): 40–44.

Rice, Sherry C. 1990. Technology management as an alliance issue: A review of the literature. *Washington Quarterly* 13 (Winter): 219–235.

Rogers, E. M. 1983. *Diffusion of innovations*. New York: Free Press.

Rogers, E. M. and F. Shoemaker. 1971. *Communication of innovation*, 2d ed. New York: Free Press.

Roiter, Alexis S. 1990. The dilemma between technology transfer promotion and control. Ph.D. dissertation, George Mason University.

Sandole, Dennis J. D. 1991. The conflict prevention centre: Prospects for cooperative conflict resolution in the new Europe. Paper for the conference on the future of pan-European institutions and CSBMs. International Institute for Peace, Vienna, 9–10 March.

Shinn, Allen M., Jr. 1990. Science, technology, and free speech. *Issues in Science and Technology* 6 (Summer): 28–31.

Tonelson, Alan. 1991. What is the national interest? *The Atlantic* (268): 35–52.

Tornatsky, Louis G. et al. 1983. *The process of technological innovation: Reviewing the literature*. Washington, DC: National Science Foundation.

Twiss, Brian. 1986. *Managing technology and innovation*, 3d ed. New York: Pittman Publishers.

U.S. Central Intelligence Agency. 1985. *White paper, Soviet acquisition of militarily significant western technologies: An update*. Washington, DC: U.S. Central Intelligence Agency.

U.S. Congress. House. Subcommittee on Science, Research, and Technology. *Technology transfer*. 99th Cong., 1st Sess., 21 and 22 May. Testimony by Bruce Merrifield.

U.S. Congress. Senate. Subcommittee on Commerce, Science, and Transportation. *New technologies on economic competitiveness*. 99th Cong., 1st Sess., 17 April, 7 May, and 1 July. Testimony by Lionel Olmer, Donald Riegle, and Richard H. Thompson.

U.S. Department of Defense. 1984. *Technology transfer control program*. An annual report to the 98th Cong. 2nd sess. (February).

————. Defense Science Board. 1976. *An analysis of export controls of U.S. technology: A DoD perspective* (known as the Bucy Report). Washington, DC: U.S. Department of Defense, Defense Science Board.

Wallerstein, Michael B. with William W. Snyder, Jr. 1991. The evolution of U.S. export control policy: 1949–1989. In *Finding common ground*, National Academy of Sciences. Washington, DC: National Academy Press.

Washington Post. 1991. U.S., Soviets reach pact reducing nuclear arms. 18 July, 1A.

3 Quality and Competitiveness: The Role of the National Institute of Standards and Technology

Robert E. Chapman and Curt W. Reimann

The U.S. competitiveness problem is not new; it has been growing in importance for more than two decades. The early responses to the problem focused on increasing productivity. As the magnitude of the problem became more evident, greater emphasis was placed on technology-based solutions. It is now widely recognized that the crux of the competitiveness problem lies in the inability of U.S. industry to transform discoveries quickly into high-quality products and into processes for designing, manufacturing, marketing, and distributing such products.

In the "global marketplace," the fruits of research and development—new data, results, inventions—are easily disseminated across national borders. Increasingly, the winners in the competitiveness race are the businesses and nations that make use of those fruits most rapidly and comprehensively. Efforts under way at the National Institute of Standards and Technology and elsewhere in the United States focus on speeding up the commercial application of basic and applied research results.

If the United States is to improve its competitive position, new R&D insights must be continuously available to be used in production processes, and new production insights must be continuously fed back into R&D. In the United States, the design phase of the technology development cycle has traditionally concentrated on the features and performance of the product rather than the processes by which it will be manufactured. This sequential approach designs the product first and then tackles the job of how to produce it. If a product can be made easily, its cost will be low and, most probably, its quality high. A complex product, with many features and elements for product performance, but designed without regard to the intricacies of making it, becomes a product of high cost, questionable quality, and uncertain reliability (Gomory and Schmitt 1988).

In Japan, research, product development, and the design of manufacturing processes are carried out concurrently so that knowledge from one area can readily influence decisions made in other areas. A new concept moves back and forth among the different groups until a good design that can be easily manufactured is produced. The process involves continuous trial and error as an innovation moves from development into production. Japan has shown that this concurrent approach speeds the transformation of new discoveries into commercial products (Reich 1989).

Challenged by the successes of our most effective competitors, the United States has begun to develop an approach that stresses the benefits of cooperation. Public/private partnerships—such as Sematech, the Advanced Technology Program, and the Malcolm Baldrige National Quality Award—are becoming not only acceptable but preferable because they leverage scarce resources at both the federal and corporate levels. These partnerships have been enabled by several key pieces of legislation that assign new responsibilities to federal R&D organizations such as NIST. These responsibilities focus on promoting the transfer of federal technologies to the private sector where commercialization activities can be undertaken. The federal commitment to technology commercialization was reinforced in the recently released report, *U.S. Technology Policy*, by the president's science advisor (Bromley 1990).

THE TECHNOLOGICAL BASIS FOR COMPETITION

Infratechnologies and Generic Technologies: The Basic Building Blocks

Technology infrastructure consists of science, engineering, and technical knowledge; it also includes infratechnologies, generic technologies, technical information, and research and test facilities (Tassey 1990a). Infratechnologies consist of methods (e.g., calibration services and standard reference materials), as well as scientific and engineering data models (e.g., standard reference data). A generic technology is defined as a concept, component, or process, or the further investigation of scientific phenomena, that has the potential to be applied to a broad range of products or processes. Generic technologies are of crucial importance to product and process development because they lay the groundwork for product/process design, testing, and manufacture. An example of a generic technology is the basic design concepts and architecture of integrated circuits.

Because generic technologies have components that are nonproprietary as well as proprietary, a business will not be able to capture the full benefit of their investment in a generic technology. Consequently, businesses tend to underinvest in generic technologies. The result, in the aggregate, of these individual investment decisions, is a reduced ability to compete in the global marketplace. The previous statement is based on the observation that generic technologies often benefit an entire industry. Generic technologies are "enabling" in that they provide the basis for economies of scale, standard interfaces, as well as stimulate the entry of small technology-oriented businesses into the industry.

Key Providers of Infratechnologies and Generic Technologies

Technology infrastructure in the Udnited States is provided by a combination of academia, industry, the public sector, and joint public-private research consortia. One key provider is the nation's system of federal laboratories. These laboratories contribute to basic scientific knowledge and the development of early-phase applied research; they account for more than $20 billion of the nation's R&D budget. Executive Order 12591 directs the federal laboratories to facilitate access to federally funded technologies, and it enables the federal laboratories to embark upon a wide range of commercially relevant research, which should increase the rate of technology acquisition (e.g., patents and licenses) and adaptation (e.g., design for manufacturability) by the private sector.

The decade of the 1980s produced several key pieces of legislation aimed at transferring the results of federally funded research to the private sector. The National Cooperative Research Act of 1984 made possible the formation of industrial research consortia and the Technology Transfer Act of 1986 allowed federal laboratories to participate in these consortia. The Technology Transfer Act also provides financial incentives to government scientists and engineers to patent technology with commercial potential and to pursue licensing of these patents. The Omnibus Trade and Competitiveness Act of 1988 added several new mechanisms for providing technology infrastructure.

The NIST Mission

As currently configured, NIST's mission is twofold: (1) the development of measurement-related technologies; and (2) technology transfer.[1] Measurement-related technologies have formed the backbone of NIST's

R&D program for nearly 90 years. To conduct basic research efficiently, measurement methods must be available that allow scientists to accurately determine the results of an experiment and communicate research results to potential users. Critically evaluated data bases, such as those provided through NIST's Standard Reference Data Program, are essential to many private-sector R&D programs. Similar requirements exist for measurement methods and data bases when generic technology research is undertaken.

Technology transfer became a high-priority issue once it was realized that technology acquisition and adaptation were neither automatic nor easily accomplished. Through the Trade Act, NIST was assigned new responsibilities focusing on the technology transfer issue.

TECHNOLOGY TRANSFER: THE HIDDEN DIMENSION OF COMPETITIVENESS

Challenges and Opportunities

Large businesses generally have the resources to acquire and adapt the technologies they need, although they may neglect to take what they could from outside the firm. For many of America's smaller businesses, exposure to new technologies is not systematic, and the effort to keep informed is often beyond their means.

To contribute to the competitiveness of U.S. industry, smaller businesses need to keep up with new technologies as much as large ones. While smaller businesses are usually not heavily involved in foreign markets themselves, their performance is important to the ability of larger ones, who are their customers, to compete. As specifications become more exacting, and the tolerance for defects decreases, the demands for smaller businesses to use new technologies grows. To better address these needs, large businesses can transfer technology to smaller businesses through partnering. Several of the recipients of the Baldrige Award have stressed the benefits of partnering with their suppliers. By working with a smaller number of "preferred" suppliers, both parties can enter into longer term relationships that result in a more complete sharing of technical information and know-how.

One way to improve the assimilation of new technology is to link publicly funded R&D to commercial production. The most adept U.S. competitors, Japan and Germany, have broad, deep institutions that support technology diffusion and transfer to smaller businesses. Although Japan is spending more on basic research than in previous years, most of its R&D efforts are aimed at rapid commercialization. One of its explicit goals is to help small and medium-sized businesses adapt new technologies. The government operates a network of 169 consulting and research centers (called *Kohsetsushi*) specifically charged with providing technical assistance to small and medium-sized businesses. The central government absorbs half of the cost, regional authorities and the businesses served pay the rest. The United States in contrast, has only a few well-established state programs and, until recently, very little at the federal level (Shapira 1990).

Technology Transfer Programs at NIST

All of the technology transfer programs at NIST have a common goal: to promote the competitive position of U.S. industry in world commerce (Kramer 1991). Many of NIST's traditional technology transfer programs involve collaborative studies in which NIST and industry join forces to solve a specific problem facing industry. These programs were significantly expanded by the Trade Act. New programs created included the Advanced Technology Program, the Manufacturing Technology Centers Program, and the State Technology Extension Program. The Trade Act also expanded the perspective of the Malcolm Baldrige National Quality Award Program by stressing the linkage between quality and competitiveness.

The Manufacturing Technology Centers Program is intended to accelerate the transfer of manufacturing technology to smaller businesses. Each center disseminates scientific, engineering, technical, and management information about manufacturing to industrial organizations within its region. To date, the technologies transferred have emphasized those developed at NIST, including NIST's Automated Manufacturing Research Facility (AMRF).

The increasing complexity of new manufacturing technologies is causing buyers to encounter high levels of uncertainty in assessing vendors' claims for product performance. In the case of systems technologies, the situation is even more complex because interfaces between components of the system are of critical importance. Demonstrations, using sample shop floor layouts at the centers and the AMRF, reduce risks to buyers by providing information on individual components as well as on systems integration.

The State Technology Extension Program is intended to improve the use of technology, particularly federal technology, by smaller businesses. This is accomplished by working through existing state and local extension activities. Currently, NIST is providing technology assistance to extension services throughout the United States; assistance includes developing workshops and seminars on technological issues and providing increased access and utilization to available NIST services (e.g., NIST's Standard Reference Data Program).

Getting technology to those who need it is one part of promoting the competitiveness of U.S. industry. Another part is ensuring that quality is built into products and services. Thousands of U.S. businesses are using the criteria from the Malcolm Baldrige National Quality Award as a mechanism for linking quality and competitiveness. The criteria, developed by NIST in conjunction with the private sector, are helping businesses to determine what they must do to meld efficiency, flexibility, quality, and innovation into their operations.

Because NIST is the primary federal laboratory with an explicit mission to aid U.S. industry, the "new" programs place NIST in a unique position to deal with the competitiveness problem. First, the new programs rest on a solid technical foundation. Consequently, NIST, in directing its outreach efforts to U.S. industry, can draw on a wide variety of scientific and technical resources. Second, the potential for synergism between the new programs and the scientific and technical research base at NIST is significant. NIST has consistently demonstrated a strong commitment to collaborative research—some efforts, such as one with the American Dental Association, have been in operation for more than 50 years.

PROMOTING COMPETITION THROUGH COLLABORATION

The New Emphasis on Collaboration

The importance of cooperative research is driven by the desire to shorten the technology development cycle. Businesses must begin to rely on external sources of technical knowledge to complement their internal R&D efforts. Businesses are cooperating on R&D-related projects in order to increase their generic technology base and to overcome the excessive cost and time lag associated with internal efforts. Even more important for future competitiveness is the recent trend toward industry-level collaboration for generic technology research.

Over the past several years, state programs designed to assist smaller businesses have increased dramatically. Currently, nearly every state has one or more programs that provide financial or technical assistance. Results from a nationwide survey conducted by NIST in collaboration with the National Governors' Association found that approximately $620 million was spent in 1988 (Chapman, Clarke, and Dobson 1990). Most states recognize the importance of technology-based competition and have initiated a variety of programs to assist businesses. For example, nearly three-quarters of all the state programs provide some form of technology assistance (e.g., product design/evaluation). The businesses served are primarily small manufacturers with two-thirds having less than 50 employees. State efforts recognize the synergy between their programs and certain federal programs. The results of the NIST survey indicate that states strongly support public/private technology development efforts, such as the Small Business Innovation Research program. State-supported SBIR programs are aimed specifically at the gap in early-stage funding. In fact, many states assist small businesses with their SBIR proposals. Several states have also initiated "bridge" programs that enable successful businesses to continue their research while awaiting the arrival of follow-on federal funding or while seeking venture capital for scale-up and market testing.

The Advanced Technology Program (ATP)

The previous discussion serves to illustrate how behavior on the part of businesses, consortia, the states, and our competitors point to the presence of a gap in early-stage funding for generic technologies. An important part of the problem is due to the "public good" nature of generic technologies, whereby a single business or industry may not be able to capture the full benefits of its investment in generic technologies. The federal government must therefore take a more active role if the bias that leads to underinvestment in generic technologies is to be removed. Industry, if left on its own, may not undertake research in key technologies that have a strong generic technology component, thus leading to a further erosion of competitiveness.

The ATP assists U.S. businesses to improve their competitive position and promote economic growth by accelerating the development of a variety of precompetitive generic technologies by means of cooperative research agreements. These agreements are funding instruments to provide financial assistance when substantial involvement is anticipated between the government and the recipient.

Research and development activities cover a wide spectrum, from basic research at one extreme to the development of specific new products at the other. The ATP is intended to foster the development of technology that is beyond basic research, but not close to the stage of new product development. Thus the ATP will include the development of laboratory prototypes intended to establish technical feasibility but not prototypes of commercial products; it will not fund projects to demonstrate commercial viability or projects involving market testing of products.

While it is hoped and intended that new products will ultimately result from work funded by the ATP, the program will not focus on giving participants a competitive advantage for new products. Rather, the focus will be on supporting work that has great economic potential with broad benefits. Accordingly, research consortia were emphasized in the Trade Act when the ATP was established. Furthermore, the ATP with its technical base of support at NIST will ensure that the limited federal funds will be used effectively to encourage and leverage private sources of support for developing generic technologies.

The ATP, by emphasizing the role of research consortia to promote the development of generic technologies, serves to increase the expected efficiency of technology transfer. Direct contact is acknowledged as the most efficient mechanism for technology transfer, and this occurs by definition during cooperative research. If participants set up complementary R&D programs within their own organizations (i.e., they emphasize technology adaptation rather than technology acquisition), transfer is even more rapid and efficient.

THE EMERGING ROLE OF QUALITY

Quality in the Global Marketplace

In the 1980s, quality was recognized as a major competitive factor. Although quality previously had been defined as conforming to specifications and/or fitness for use, the current working definition of quality is becoming broader in that service factors are now included as well as product specifications. Quality is now more operational- or organizational-oriented in that concepts such as continuous improvement and prevention are viewed as the dominant drivers. Strategic quality objectives have taken on a "systems" approach in that continuous improvement is sought in service levels, delivery, products, and production capability. Operationally, this evolution is evident by a change from the narrow focus on inspection to one of prevention (Tassey 1990b).

Another way of understanding the new concept of quality to businesses is to list the four stages in the evolution of quality management (Peach 1991): (1) Inspection—quality is inspected in; (2) Statistical Quality Control—quality is controlled in; (3) Quality Assurance—quality is built in; and (4) Strategic Quality Management—quality is managed in. During the same period, management responsibilities increased from one of chief inspector to one of chief quality officer. The evolution shows that quality has become an integral part of business operations. The elevation of quality issues to senior management demonstrates the need for a systems approach in order to achieve results.

The Malcolm Baldrige National Quality Award

The Malcolm Baldrige National Quality Improvement Act of 1987 created an annual quality award for the United States. The purposes of the Baldrige Award are threefold: promote quality awareness, recognize quality achievements of U.S. businesses, and publicize successful quality strategies. There are three categories for Awards: manufacturing, service, and small business (i.e., businesses with less than 500 employees). Up to two Awards may be given in each category each year, and recipients may publicize and advertise based on their Awards.

Awards are made on the basis of a three-stage review process: (1) evaluation of written examinations submitted by applicants, (2) site visits to applicants that score high on the written examination to review strengths and areas for improvement as revealed in the written examination, and (3) final judging of overall results—written examinations and site visit reports.

The written examination plays a central role in the Award process. The Award criteria, which form the basis of the written examination, define a framework for total quality management (TQM). The framework comprises four main elements: the "goal", the "driver" of the system, the system itself, and measures of progress. The examination designed to meet these requirements consists of seven categories: leadership, information and analysis, strategic quality planning, human resource utilization, quality assurance of products and services, quality results, and customer satisfaction. Within the seven categories, examination items address key diagnostic indicators of excellence and continuity that, taken together, project the value system for TQM. The Award criteria are an important adjunct of the examination. They not only are the basis for assessing Award applicants, but also represent an extension of the examination's value system. The criteria are particularly important in projecting the meaning of "total" in total quality management. Annual updates of the Award criteria are through a consensus process to ensure that the value system evolves as learning takes place (i.e., through continuous improvement) (Reimann 1989).

The Award criteria were designed to provide a complete profile of each applicant's overall quality management. This feature makes it adaptable for uses other than the Award competition. Because the Award criteria were designed as a value system, they are adaptable to the needs of any organization. Currently, the Award criteria are being used throughout the United States in four basic areas—assessment, setting up a quality system, communications, and education and training.

Lessons Learned from the Baldrige Award

Much has been learned since the Baldrige Award was created in 1987. First, the Award criteria have become a vehicle for change for those who are serious about quality excellence. Second, because the Award recipients serve as models for others, they demonstrate that what was possible for them is possible for others. The following are highlights of what has been learned in the first four years of the Award program.

Many of the "lessons learned" are summarized in a report by the U.S. General Accounting Office (GAO) (1991). The objective of the GAO study was to determine the impact of formal TQM practices on the performance of selected U.S. businesses. The GAO report focused on: (1) what was achieved by adopting these practices, (2) how improved quality was achieved, and (3) what lessons may be applicable to U.S. businesses in general.

The GAO study reviewed data and other information on 20 businesses that were the highest-scoring applicants in 1988 and 1989 for the Baldrige Award. Results presented in the GAO report show that TQM is useful for smaller businesses as well as large ones and for businesses that sell services as well as for those that sell manufactured products. The GAO study showed that adopting TQM as a method for conducting their business had a positive impact on corporate performance. These results indicate that TQM systems are promising ways to strengthen competitiveness of a business in both domestic and world markets.

An important finding of the GAO study was that some features of TQM are widely applicable to other organizations and could result in improved performance. Several of these important features are summarized below.

- Customer satisfaction is critical in order to remain competitive in the marketplace. Ultimately, customer satisfaction, both internal and external, drives quality efforts. Organizations, therefore, need to determine what customers want and must have processes in place to meet those customer needs.

- Top executives must provide active leadership to establish quality as a fundamental value to be incorporated into the corporate management philosophy. Top executives need to establish a corporate culture that involves all employees in contributing to quality improvements. Quality concepts need to be clearly articulated and thoroughly integrated throughout all activities of the business.

- Businesses need to focus on employee involvement, teamwork, and training at all levels. This focus should strengthen employee commitment to continuous quality improvement.

- Suppliers should be made full partners in the quality management process. A close working relationship between suppliers and producers could be mutually beneficial.

To succeed, TQM systems must be based on a continuous and systematic approach of gathering, evaluating, and acting on facts and data.

The published results show that a TQM approach based on the Baldrige Award criteria has a positive impact on the "bottom line." Among the recipients of the Baldrige Award, this is especially true. In the case of Motorola, it has gone from a business under threat to one where it is the chief threat to competitors. Most of its products have increased their market share, here and abroad. In Japan, for example, Motorola pagers, supplied to Nippon Telephone and Telegraph, were introduced in 1982 and now claim a major share of that market. In addition to its success in the Japanese market, Motorola has achieved impressive cost savings due to the Six Sigma Initiative. These cost savings are due to four commonly used measures that have a direct impact on the bottom line, specifically, reductions in scrap rates, rework costs, warranty costs, and inventory holding costs. Motorola estimates that cumulative cost savings have exceeded $1 billion since launching the Six Sigma Initiative in 1987.

Other recipients of the Baldrige Award have also experienced favorable impacts on their bottom line. Xerox Corporation's Business Products and Systems received the Baldrige Award in 1989. They are currently targeting a 50 percent reduction in unit manufacturing cost and a fourfold improvement in reliability by 1993. Globe Metallurgical, the 1988 Small Business Award recipient, increased its annual sales by 30 percent in 1988. The Wallace Company, the 1990 Small Business Award recipient, has scored impressive gains on a number of fronts. Since 1987, Wallace's market share has increased from 10.4 percent to 18 percent. Its record of on-time deliveries has jumped from 75 percent in 1987 to well in excess of 90 percent. As a result, sales volume has grown 69 percent and, because of greater efficiency, operating profits increased 7.4 times.

Probably the most important lesson of all is that extremely high-quality targets are attainable with the right strategies and enough will. The quality targets for the Baldrige Award, it should be stressed, are not relative—they are absolute. The aim is nothing less than excellence. Businesses speak of "zero defects in everything we do," "total customer satisfaction," and being "the best." Once a business has won a Baldrige Award, it continues to pursue aggressive quality goals. Businesses that adopt such an approach are dealing with the competitiveness issue head on. Continuous improvement and listening to the "voice of the customer" become the new drivers for the innovation process.

CONCLUDING REMARKS

Efficiency in production is absolutely essential to long-term market success. The original superior performance attributes of the innovator's product are often rapidly imitated, frequently at lower cost and higher quality. Investments in superior process technologies have often been the difference. At the core of such an approach are a range of measurement-related technologies that are increasingly integrated into the process technologies. Current activities at NIST place special emphasis on such integration/interface issues.

By studying and then emulating the Baldrige Award criteria, U.S. businesses have begun to: (1) broaden their definitions of quality to include virtually all business activities; and (2) include the implementation of quality assurance strategies in their interactions with materials and equipment suppliers. These "lessons learned" are resulting in new initiatives with aggressive quality goals. By taking an aggressive approach to quality issues, U.S. businesses are forced to move away from the inefficient sequential approach to the technology development cycle—R&D, engineering, production, and distribution—to the concurrent approach. Furthermore, the emphasis on service quality as a differentiating mechanism and on total customer satisfaction should stimulate innovation and result in a shorter technology development cycle.

In the long run, the ability of U.S. industry to compete successfully also depends on the contributions of technology infrastructure. Experiences over the past decade suggest that Japan may simply have more of such infrastructure to offer its businesses. This may be true for Germany and other European countries as well. Thus, NIST efforts aimed at providing an efficient technology infrastructure that creates, consolidates, and transfers certain types of widely used information, including much that is related to quality improvement, may make a decided difference.

NOTE

1. Technology transfer is defined here as the process by which technology, knowledge, or information developed in one organization, in one area, or for one purpose is applied and utilized in another organization, in another area, or for another purpose.

REFERENCES

Bromley, D. Allan. 1990. *U.S. technology policy*. Washington, DC: Executive Office of the President.

Chapman, Robert E., Marianne K. Clarke, and Eric Dobson. 1990. *Technology-based economic development: A study of state and federal technical extension services*. Gaithersburg, MD: National Institute of Standards and Technology. NIST Special Publication 786.

Gomory, Ralph E. and Roland W. Schmitt. 1988. Science and product. *Science* (May): 1131–1132.

Kramer, Samuel. 1991. Old or new, NIST's technology transfer programs promote U.S. position in world commerce. *ASME News* 10 (9):8.

Peach, Robert W. 1991. Creating a pattern of excellence. *Quality Digest* (April): 69–83.

Reich, Robert B. 1989. The quiet path to technological preeminence. *Scientific American* (October): 41–47.

Reimann, Curt W. 1989. The Baldrige award: Leading the way in quality initiatives. *Quality Progress* (July): 35–39.

Shapira, Philip. 1990. *Modernizing manufacturing: New policies to build industrial extension services*. Washington, DC: Economic Policy Institute.

Tassey, Gregory. 1990a. *The functions of technology infrastructure in a competitive economy*. Gaithersburg, MD: National Institute of Standards and Technology.

————— 1990b. *Investment in quality and U.S. competitiveness*. Gaithersburg, MD: National Institute of Standards and Technology.

U.S. General Accounting Office. 1991. *Management practices: U.S. companies improve performance through quality efforts*. Washington, DC: U.S. General Accounting Office. GAO/NSIAD-91–190.

4 Thinking Spinoffs in the 1990s: The Emerging Role of the Department of Defense in Technology Transfer

James A. Ball

Why is it that the Japanese and other nations can take the fruits of U.S. knowledge and innovation and create products long before our industry can? Why is it that, although the United States plows billions of dollars into research and development through federal programs, so little of it gets to the marketplace in a timely manner? How much longer can we watch U.S. technology leak offshore only to show up as competition for U.S. domestic industry at the cost of jobs and a reduced standard of living? One of the major factors contributing to the degradation of U.S. economic competitiveness in the international arena is the national propensity to ignore the value of the technology that we evolve through federal R&D programs. Although effective technology transfer processes can be vital to the U.S. international competitive posture, they are not recognized for their potential. High tech product and process opportunities languish because they are not perceived as valuable by either U.S. federal agencies or industry.

There are many aspects of the "competitiveness" issue in addition to the technology factor: quality technical education, product quality, conservation of resources, and the balance of national priorities for maintaining national security interests while increasing the national standard of living. Of the many issues involved in competitiveness, new technology continues to emerge as a key element. The Department of Defense alone manages over two thirds of the federal budget for research and development (Brooks and Branscomb 1989). While it is true that most of this funding goes for development, and some will argue that most of that has little utility elsewhere, it still contributes to the advancement of technology though the experience of U.S. scientists and engineers, and along with the funding for basic and advanced research makes a large contribution to the national technology resource. Thus, given the fact that the Department of Defense is, and most likely will remain, a key driver of the technology base of the nation, it has to be considered a prime player in the arena of technology transfer.

SWORDS TO PLOWSHARES—FACT OR FANTASY?

Many questions surround the technology transfer issue. Is it possible to beat defense swords into economic plowshares and convert defense technology into civilian applications? Is it practical? Has defense technology become too exotic to have application elsewhere? What of the forecast decline for defense-related R&D? History has shown that commercialization of defense technology is not only possible and practical, but also traditional—it is something that has been going on for centuries.

The practicality of defense-related spinoffs is often challenged from the standpoint that it would be much more efficient to develop the spinoff directly. The simplicity of this argument does not consider that defense R&D is not intended to develop spinoffs, nor should it be. The practicality issue is not part of the equation; spinoffs from defense technology are by definition a by-product and an unanticipated benefit of the investment in maintaining national security. The wisdom of this investment was recently reaffirmed in the Persian Gulf war.

The "practicality" question often generates discussion of the "best mix" of military funding of basic versus applied R&D that will result in the most spinoffs. This mix has never been considered from this perspective by DOD because of its mission orientation. This perspective may be changing, however, in the wake of changes in Europe and the Persian Gulf War. In a recent review of this and other issues confronting the defense technical community, the Carnegie Commission (1990) concluded that the DOD must "learn how to share in technological advances" and, in doing so, must consider sustaining basic and applied research at the expense of development. The Commission recommended such measures as building up a "reserve" of technical concepts and designs that could keep a wide range of advanced technology options "warm." Consideration of this approach, along with other measures that reduce the barriers to DOD use of commercial technology, are potential solutions to the current challenge—approaches that may be able to keep the U.S. technologically secure as well as provide a more productive environment for spinoffs and economic viability.

Returning to the question of possibility, technical advances in defense technology have, throughout history, contributed greatly to the advancement of science and innovation, but the origins of many of these advancements is seldom recognized. Examples include microwave ovens, developed from military radar, and Corning's Photogray™ spectacle lenses commercialized from a once-classified material developed for the windshield of the B-58 bomber to protect crew members against nuclear weapon flash. Derivatives of turbosuperchargers originally developed for fighter aircraft in World War II now power our high-performance automobiles; Magnetic Resonance Imaging used throughout the country for medical diagnostic work evolved from naval anti-submarine warfare equipment; and many vaccines and medicines that have eliminated diseases throughout the world were developed to protect and treat U.S. forces deployed in past conflicts.

Has military technology become so sophisticated and exotic today that it has no application to other uses? The answer, based on the past five years of advancements coming from the Strategic Defense Initiative (SDI), is a resounding No! While it is true that these technologies are sophisticated and exotic, their applications are meeting needs from the simplistic to the profound. New SDI-funded advanced materials processes are now used to make engine bearings for automobiles that will double engine life. Similar processes have been applied to end products ranging from prosthetic braces twice as strong and half the weight of conventional braces to construction equipment wear surfaces that last five times longer than current steel materials. The sensors for air bags in automobiles come from two sources: either Army artillery fuze technology or a new SDI sensor technology developed for space-based interceptor systems. In the medical arena, direct derivatives of small particle accelerators designed for SDI-directed energy weapons are now in use treating cancer at a hospital in Loma Linda, California; magnetic suspension technology designed to test an SDI space interceptor evolved into a device now being tested to conduct cataract surgery; and SDI free electron laser technology has been in use for over five years as a key research tool in medical applications that include kidney and gallstone ablation, removal of plaque in arteries, and treatment of whole blood to rid it of AIDS, hepatitis, and herpes viruses.

With the explosion of new technology coming at an ever-increasing rate, it is logical to predict that the applications of military technology to other uses will certainly not decline in the next decade unless defense R&D also declines. If it does, and is not replaced in any other R&D sector that is broad-based in nature, the U.S. technology base may also decline and, with it, the opportunity to remain technically competitive in world markets.

OPPORTUNITY IN THE COMING DECADE

With the potential decline of technological competitiveness and its impact on the economy, it is opportune to examine several recent government reports that reveal a good deal about technology and investment strategy for the decade of the 1990s. Two of these reports outline the technical priorities for the U.S. economy as well as for U.S. national security. They offer a vivid insight about our national technical and economic priorities and the issues surrounding them, especially the potential for technology transfer from Department of Defense R&D.

First, the economic perspective. The Department of Commerce recently issued a report on Emerging Technologies (U.S. Department of Commerce 1990) describing 12 technology areas that, in the next ten years, DOC predicts will be worth some $356 billion dollars in domestic revenue, and over a trillion dollars in international commerce if Americans can capitalize on their own innovation. The report provides a road map on how these technologies can be employed to enhance U.S. competitiveness and presents the challenge in terms of the international competition. The report assesses how the United States stands in the state-of-the-art in these 12 technical areas with respect to other countries.

Almost in synchronization with the Commerce Report, the Department of Defense published its second annual Critical Technologies report (U.S. Department of Defense 1990). The report outlined 22 technologies that are critical to defense needs and the priority in which the Defense Department intends to make investment in the 1990s. Remembering that the DOD spends some two-thirds of the federal R&D budget, it seems useful to take a look at how these reports overlap and where researchers, entrepreneurs, corporations, and investors might want to target their efforts. If DOD's investment strategy in the critical technologies is overlaid with what the Department of Commerce predicts is going to drive the economy, one can see the congruence of defense investment and economic opportunity (see Figure 4.1). This indicates the extreme importance of concentrating on doing something meaningful and productive about moving DOD technology, as it is generated, into the U.S. industrial sector. It is imperative that applicable technology be commercialized to spur our economy at the same time it is being applied to our defense needs. The effort needs to be now, and not follow the traditional path that starts years or decades from now.

After the DOD and DOC reports became available, the White House Office of Science and Technology Policy commissioned a panel to review these and other independent reports on critical and emerging technologies. The panel produced a report that consolidated the information and created

Figure 4.1
Comparison of Technology Priorities

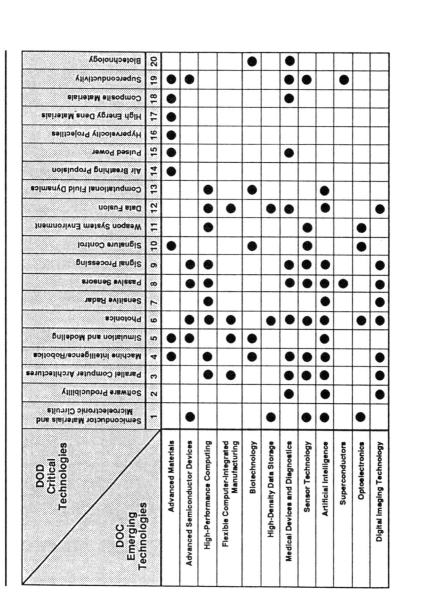

a basic road map for technological investment (U.S. Office of Science and Technology Policy 1991). At the same time that the OSTP report was released, the Department of Defense issued an updated version of the Critical Technologies Plan, which provides extensive information relating the critical technologies to actual military programs and systems (U.S. Department of Defense 1991a). These two recent documents provide an even more detailed picture of the linkages of military program technology to the potential impact on the economy.

THE CHALLENGES OF MOVING TECHNOLOGY

There are many barriers to moving technology from its original use to secondary application, and some of them are in place for good reason. The technology transfer process is intellectual and thus is a personal interaction process. Information systems and data bases are tools that enable the process, but technology transfer is not a data-to-person process; it requires the personal contact element. Federal technology transfer programs require responsive methodologies—ways that are easy to use, accessible to the maximum number of people, and provided at minimum cost. Federal technology transfer programs must be proactive; the technology must be identified, pushed, and "latched up" with the market pull. Finally, there must be a means of tracking and a following up to assure that the barriers are overcome and that commercialization does not stall.

Natural Barriers

Natural barriers to technology transfer abound. There are many issues involved with the transfer of intellectual property. One is the time it takes to get a patent, the legal hassles, and the other negotiations that have to take place in any kind of an intellectual property scenario. The intellectual property process often intimidates and impedes the entrepreneurial process and seemingly takes forever. Another problem is that many people in small businesses who would like to use technology have an abhorrence of bureaucracies. They look at any government bureaucracy as a monolith that is difficult to penetrate and communicate with. The recent federal procurement laws and adversarial attitudes that they create between government and industry contribute to the further inhibition of the entrepreneur who could best use new technology.

Overcoming the bureaucratic barrier is a key role for state, local, and regional management and technical assistance organizations. These organizations are sometimes unrecognized yet vital communications links between small business and large government, with a great potential for success. They are particularly helpful in cases where there is inadequate planning for commercialization on the part of participants in Small Business Innovation Research and similar programs. Many of these "businesses" are typically sole-proprietor inventors who are good bench scientists and engineers but not necessarily good businessman. They wind up at the end of Phase II of the SBIR process with a wonderful "widget" but no market for it, and no sponsor to turn the innovation into a commercial product. This problem, combined with a traditional lack of seed and investment capital for the transition of the project from prototype to an actual marketable project, is one of the greatest barriers to successful commercialization of technology.

Cultural Barriers

Aside from the natural barriers, getting technology out of the Department of Defense is compounded by "cultural" barriers unique to the DOD community. Much of the problem is due to perspective. Many individuals in DOD view the definition of "technology transfer" as giving national secrets away. In fact, the words "technology transfer" in the titles or missions of most DOD organizations are attributed to offices and agencies that are chartered to inhibit or prohibit technology transfer, not to enable it. The positive technology transfer connotation given recently to DOD programs is "domestic technology transfer." This connotation differentiates these activities from those that are chartered to inhibit international technology transfer.

These security-oriented barriers are in place for good reason. Just before Iraq invaded Kuwait in 1990, two high-temperature industrial furnaces that the Iraqis purchased from a U.S. company were in the process of being shipped. The Iraqis ostensibly wanted these furnaces to produce prosthetics for their handicapped war veterans (*Science* 1991). The Department of Commerce granted an export license (apparently without DOD coordination) and the furnaces were sitting on the dock ready to go aboard a ship to Iraq when U.S. Customs blew the whistle. It turned out that the Iraqis had ordered four of these furnaces, including two more from a Scottish subsidiary of the U.S. company, and intended to use them to produce nuclear weapons devices! This event happened just a few years after the "technology transfer" of high tech numerically controlled manufacturing equipment that enabled the Soviets to produce more silent-running submarines. Add to this the very remarkable resemblance of the Soviet-built space shuttle and front-line combat aircraft to their U.S. counterparts and it is obvious why technology transfer controls are in place and why there is a negative connotation on technology transfer in the DOD community.

Unfortunately, the application of controls usually is traditionally over-done because of DOD concentration on "negative" tech transfer; therefore, much of what is published on technology transfer from DOD is negative. The mind-set continually reinforced is that all DOD technology is sensitive and must be protected. Compounding this factor is the perspective that many DOD people think it is a conflict of interest and perhaps illegal to provide government technology to business interests. As to any positive perspective of tech transfer in DOD, it is usually limited to providing technical data to a restricted community of qualified DOD contractors with little or no emphasis on personal interaction.

The barriers to tech transfer at DOD center around the issues of security and export control. DOD personnel tend to think of most technical matters as sensitive—either classified, or on the Militarily Critical Technology List (MCTL). They also sometimes confuse the two. Classification is a process that often gets mistakenly extended from the real or potential ability of a new weapon system to meet a classified threat to the subsystems and components in the weapon system itself. Add to this the misperception that if a technology is contained in the MCTL it cannot be exported, and you have a formidable bureaucratic process that inhibits the flow of technology.

Another unfortunate aspect is that the security barrier not only inhibits the sharing of technology outside of the DOD, it inhibits the sharing among DOD agencies themselves. A technology listed on the MCTL means that the concern is there that the technology may have the potential to be used against us, not that it is a foregone conclusion that it can and will. What MCTL listing means is simply that a listed technology warrants review on a case-by-case basis before it can be exported. Unfortunately, most DOD personnel have a tendency to confuse these issues and don't understand the difference between them. Actually, the export control provisions can be used to enable access by U.S. corporations instead of inhibiting it. This methodology was successfully used in designing the SDI Technology Applications Program. The MCTL system works for controlled, positive technology transfer to U.S. industry through provisions that permit access by U.S. companies to the technology. The list of certified companies is also used to market the availability of the new technology via directed mailings to promote interest in commercialization. The SDI Technology Applications Program actually facilitates access to its new technology through use of the MCTL certification process. This access is enabled by a modem-accessible information system that is designed to bring U.S. citizens and corporations together with SDI researchers while protecting intellectual property rights and national security.

Another barrier is the documentation and accessibility of DOD technology. The DOD operates the Defense Technical Information Center (DTIC) to receive, catalog, and store defense technology information. DTIC is a $30 million-a-year operation that provides information only to current DOD contractors (with the exception of bidders on SBIR programs). The information channel is restricted to DOD contractors, sophisticated, expensive to use, and contains incomplete and dated information on DOD research and development. Information is usually provided in lengthy computer report formats that are laborious to review and do not necessarily offer an active linkage with someone who is actually doing current research. The documentation system is further complicated by the fact that many DOD R&D agencies do not enter data into the system in a timely fashion.

While success of technology transfer in the DOD is thus limited by the institutional mind-set and culture, this is not a unique situation to the DOD. Cultural perspectives on technology transfer vary among federal agencies. To illustrate, it is interesting to look at the perspective of the medical research community associated with the National Institutes of Health (NIH). Before the Federal Technology Transfer Act (FTTA) of 1986, academically oriented NIH scientists shared the fruits of their research freely with non profit organizations, universities, and industry without regard to the legalities of patents and license agreements. With the advent of the FTTA, scientists and researchers were burdened with a bureaucratic process that they found to be complicated, poorly understood, and too legalistic. Most of the scientific community reacted with a "too hard to work" attitude toward the FTTA requirements and continue to believe that this new legislated bureaucracy hinders technology transfer, scientific research, and the free exchange of ideas in an academic environment.

Along with the changes in the military threat that ushered in the '90s, there is also a profound change in the global technology base that has two strong implications for DOD technology policy. Not only does the nation need to do a better job of moving DOD related technology to commercial applications, DOD must also draw upon the commercial technology base for much of its need. Unfortunately, the same cultural attitudes regarding outward technology transfer mentioned previously also impede the infusion of technology into Defense programs (Carnegie Commission 1990). If DOD is to have better access to new emerging technology in the private sector, the same barriers must be breached.

PROGRESS AND PROMISE

Although the barriers to the access of DOD technology are formidable, progress is being made. Attitudes are starting to change. The Federal Technology Transfer Act of 1986 was instituted by a Department of Defense directive almost three years after the passage of the law. The directive contains all the right words: encourage dissemination, promote sharing, share profits, stimulate industry, exchange new ideas, and so on. The directive emphatically states that it is now the mission of all those involved in the R&D efforts in the DOD to engage in technology transfer. The directive recognizes the need for a new attitude that can be referred to as "Think Spinoffs." It is a state of mind that everyone from researchers to top-level managers in the technology community needs to adopt; a mind-set that proactively considers uses of technology beyond the original application.

The Federal Technology Act authorizes and advocates the use of Cooperative Research and Development Agreements (CRDAs) between federal laboratories and industry to enable technology transfer. These CRDA vehicles are becoming a primary success factor in moving technology from the federal laboratories. The law provides for royalties to the laboratory personnel who develop new inventions for commercialization and allows the use of laboratory resources—facilities, staff, and know-how—with private sector funding.

Along with CRDAs, the government is recognizing the power of other mechanisms ranging from directed university research projects in high tech investment areas to federally sponsored consortia to enhance our national technology base. Examples are DOD's recent sponsorship of some 16 Centers of Excellence in DOD related areas (U.S. General Accounting Office 1990); the Defense Advanced Research Project Agency's programs for HDTV, X-ray Lithography, strategic computing, and the newly established DOD program for advanced manufacturing technology. This precompetitive technology development program opens the door for consortia arrangements sponsored by DOD (Richards 1990) that provide excellent vehicles for commercialization.

THE SERVICES RESPOND

Among the military services, the Air Force deserves recognition for publishing an implementing regulation in early 1990, and for developing it in even stronger language than in the DOD directive. The regulation states that it is the mission of all Air Force R&D agencies and their personnel to engage in technology transfer. The Army released its regulation in June 1991. As of this writing, the Navy has not yet issued a regulation to the field to implement the FTTA.

Although technology transfer policy has been moving at glacial speed at the headquarters levels in DOD, some field activities have moved to implement the legislation and the DOD directive. The Army now has over 70 active Offices of Research and Technology Applications, 100 CRDAs have been signed by the Army, and most of this was completed in the past year.

The Navy's technology transfer efforts are somewhat low key by comparison to the other services. The Navy publishes a monthly Fact Sheet that outlines new Navy technology with dual applications that is available free to anyone who wishes to subscribe (U.S. Navy 1991). It has good examples of Navy technology and inventions, and additional information can be obtained by mailing back a card that is part of the publication. The Navy is also actively processing CRDAs with industry at its laboratories. Thirty-five CRDAs exist as of this writing and several dozen more are in process.

In 1990, the Naval Air Development Center, in conjunction with the Federal Laboratory Consortium (FLC) and SDI, initiated the Business Gold program. The program is centered on a modem-accessible data base and is a pilot project through the FLC. The system became operational on the Bell Atlantic Intelligate System in the Philadelphia area in June 1990 and can be accessed from anywhere in the world via computer modem. The Business Gold system has three basic parts: new "showcase" technology available for licensing or CRDA development from the major R&D organizations in government, sources of state technical assistance available, and small business R&D opportunities. The third aspect of Business Gold provides opportunities for small and disadvantaged businesses available throughout the government, including all the SBIR abstracts from a number of federal agencies. The near-term goal for Business Gold is to consistently provide all active federal SBIR program offerings on line.

The Air Force has some very proactive state, regional, and local technology transfer programs. There are cooperative agreements with six states where laboratories are forging solid agreements with the state and local economic development agencies to use Air Force technology to create new products and industries. The Air Force also recently published an excellent technology transfer handbook for use by all of the military services.

Tying most of the DOD technology transfer effort together is the Federal Laboratory Consortium for Technology Transfer in which the DOD laboratories play a major role. All of the major DOD laboratories are active and provide a significant portion of funding and leadership for the FLC efforts. The FLC sponsors a national clearinghouse program and a number of proactive technology transfer demonstration projects, like Business Gold, to examine new ways of moving technology from the laboratories to the marketplace.

In 1989, DOD's Defense Technology Information Center established a Domestic Technology Referral Database, a referral to laboratory experts in specific technology areas (U.S. Department of Defense 1991b). The program is designed to provide the name of an expert at one of these DOD labs who may be able to provide technical assistance in the use of a given technology. This program can go a long way toward establishing the personal interaction so vital to effective technology transfer.

Finally, a very proactive technology transfer program that is unique to the DOD is the SDI Technology Applications Program established in the same year that the Technology Transfer Act was passed. Today, SDI continues to have a technology transfer program that proactively reviews SDI-related R&D, conducts technology application reviews, captures the essence of the information of that technology into a modem accessible system known as the Technology Applications Information System (TAIS), and makes it available to U.S. citizens and industry with certified access to Militarily Critical Technology (U.S. Department of Defense 1991c). Qualified U.S. corporations, organizations, and citizens now number in excess of 18,000. The system also has, in addition to over 1,600 abstracts and referrals on new technology, the research opportunities that are available through SDI. State technology transfer assistance agencies, directories, and other sources of technology information are also available on-line. The program actively interfaces with other federal R&D agencies, industrial associations, and state and local economic development organizations to enhance the synergy of federal technology transfer activities. To illustrate the impact that SDI can have on the economy, Figure 4.2 indicates the contributions that SDI has made through FY 91 to DOD Critical Technologies and the number of technology abstracts in the SDI TAIS that correlate with the foremost commercially viable emerging technology areas outlined in the Department of Commerce report mentioned earlier.

ANOTHER PROMISING INITIATIVE

Another important technology transfer initiative is the National Technology Transfer Center, which was legislated by Congress in 1989. The Center is currently being established in Wheeling, West Virginia, and

Figure 4.2
SDI Contributions to Critical Technologies

Technology	DOD/DOE Funding	SDIO Funding	SDIO Share %	TAIS Abstracts	Technology	DOD/DOE Funding	SDIO Funding	SDIO Share %	TAIS Abstracts
Semiconductor Material, Microelectric Circuits	340	50	14.7	397	Weapon Systems Environment	170	100	58.8	1
Software Producibility	130	21	16.2	104	Data Fusion	50	10	20.0	4
Parallel Computer Architectures	120	22	18.3	27	Computational Fluid Dynamics	80	8	10.0	42
Machine Intelligence, Robotics	120	2	1.7	10	Air Breathing Propulsion	*	0	0	42
Simulation & Modeling	210	60	28.6	84	Pulsed Power	170	55	32.4	127
Photonics	100	12	12.0	13	Hypervelocity Projectiles	140	63	45.0	22
Sensitive Radars	110	45	40.9	85	High Energy Density Materials	90	30	33.3	8
Passive Sensors	460	355	77.0	10	Composite Materials	180	55	30.6	92
Signal Processing	130	45	34.6	68	Superconductivity	130	42	32.3	54
Signature Control	*	25	*	13	Biotechnology	97	6	6.2	0

*Not tabulated by SDI Office.

Note: The Information in the SDIO TAIS is available to U.S. industry to support increased productivity and competitiveness.

Source: Strategic Defense Initiative Office, February 9, 1990.

promises to serve as a single point for access to all federal technology. The Center will be several years in its establishment, but it holds great promise to serve as a facilitator and supporting element for technology transfer throughout the U.S.

THE LEGACY AND THE CHALLENGE

There is a substantial storehouse of technology that has been developed by Defense and other federal R&D programs that can make a difference in the quality of life for the nation and other people of the world. The technology is viable and applicable to numerous nondefense uses. As a nation of innovative people, we owe it to ourselves and our children to claim this technology and put it to use. The challenge is for federal government, state agencies, and industry to work together to eliminate the barriers that now inhibit this process. In doing so, there can truly be new plowshares of progress forged from the swords of defense. "Think Spin-offs—Keep America Competitive" is a slogan whose time has come.

REFERENCES

Brooks, Harvey and Lewis Branscomb. 1989. Rethinking the military's role in the economy. *Technology Review* (August-September): 54–64.

Carnegie Commission on Science, Technology and Government. 1990. *New thinking and American defense technology.* New York: Carnegie Commission.

Richards, Evelyn. 1990. Technology development fares well in budget. *Washington Post*, 30 October, 3D.

Science. 1991. War with Iraq spurs new export controls. *Science* 1 February, 4993.

U.S. Department of Commerce, Technology Administration. 1990. *Emerging technologies: A survey of technical and economic opportunities.* Washington, DC: U.S. Department of Commerce.

U.S. Department of Defense. 1990. *The Department of Defense Critical Technologies Plan for the Committees on Armed Services of the United States Congress.* Washington, DC: U.S. Department of Defense.

———. 1991a. *The Department of Defense Critical Technologies Plan.* Washington, DC: U.S. Department of Defense.

U.S. Department of Defense, Defense Technology Information Center, Office of Marketing and Product Management. 1991b. *Domestic Technology Referral Database.* Cameron Station, VA.: U.S. Department of Defense.

U.S. Department of Defense, Strategic Defense Initiative Organization, Office of Technology Applications. 1991c. *Technology Applications Information System.* Washington, DC: U.S. Department of Defense.

U.S. General Accounting Office. 1990. *Defense research: Information on selected university research projects.* Washington, DC: U.S. General Accounting Office. GAO/NSIAD-90–223FS.

U.S. Navy, Naval Surface Warfare Center. 1991. *Navy Domestic Technology Fact Sheet.* Dahlgren, VA: U.S. Navy. Code E211.

U.S. Office of Science and Technology Policy, National Critical Technologies Panel. 1991. *Report of the National Critical Technologies Panel.* Arlington, VA: U.S. Office of Science and Technology Policy.

II State Programs, Institutions, and Issues

5 The Turbulent Condition of State S&T Programs in the 1990s

W. Henry Lambright, Albert H. Teich, and Mark J. O'Gorman

In recent years, scholars and practitioners of science and technology policy have documented the profound growth in the role of the states in S&T in the 1980s (Lambright and Teich 1989; Osborne 1988; Atkinson 1991; Lambright and Rahm 1991; Schmandt and Wilson 1987). Before the past decade, apart from agriculture and short-lived initiatives in energy, most states had done little either to encourage or exploit S&T to serve their policy objectives. In the 1980s, however, due to a number of internal and external forces, many governors and legislators asserted political leadership through technology-based economic development programs. By the end of the decade, the number and variety of state S&T programs developed in the United States had made state S&T one of the nation's fastest growing and most dynamic policy areas.[1]

In the early 1990s, that optimistic description of the condition of state S&T programs can no longer be sustained. Fiscal crises in the budgets of many states, changes in political leadership, and subsequent policy reconfigurations have forced major changes in many state S&T programs. Some programs have been cut outright from their state budgets; others have had to adjust to deep budget erosion. And state S&T programs that have emerged relatively intact now question the future outlook of their programs. These fiscal problems affecting state S&T programs, changes in policy reorientation, and increasing number of political struggles within the states have changed the ambience of state S&T programs from one of unabashed optimism to one of turmoil.

Adding to this turbulence is the continued hesitancy of the U.S. federal government to become a champion for competitiveness programs in S&T. Although the Bush administration and legislators in Washington continue to call for S&T programs to revitalize U.S. industry, little momentum has been generated. The federal S&T programs that do exist are primarily state-specific and/or secondary aids to state and local S&T programs. It is clear that the federal government has allowed the leadership role in S&T competitiveness programs to fall to the states. But state governments are themselves struggling to sustain their own S&T programs.

The combination of increased fiscal mothballing of state S&T programs and continued federal hesitancy to fill this policy vacuum does present a turbulent image of state S&T programs in the 1990s. But this is *not* to say that this turbulence is pervasive in all the states. In fact, a few state S&T programs are growing and even flourishing. But what is clear is that while this turmoil is not pervasive in every state, the changing fiscal and political scene in the states in the early 1990s has had major negative impacts on most state S&T programs. Even wider variations in the range and level of S&T programs in the states now exist.

At the federal level, the initiatives in S&T already in place can provide an opportunity for Washington to become more of a leader in S&T programs. These few informal and focused federal programs have been successful. They can provide a model by which the federal government can expand and help sustain the state S&T programs through these difficult fiscal and political times. Realistically, the final policy decision will be political; and the resources available to aid the states are limited. But from an implementation standpoint, organizations and programs are in place that can allow the federal government to provide significant aid to state S&T programs.

What is true today for every state S&T program is that the initial burst of youthful energy that characterized these programs in the 1980s has faded into the fiscal and political realities of the 1990s. State S&T programs now have to struggle along with other state political institutions for survival. They must engage in political battles and fight to hold on to whatever policy niche state S&T programs have carved out for themselves. For advocates of state S&T programs, these political battles can occupy disproportionate amounts of time and resources, distracting them from their ultimate goals.

What does this mean for S&T programs in the states? Is this just a short-term problem, symptomatic of the current economic downturn? Or is this the beginning of a more sustained period of turbulence for these programs? Some of the same S&T programs that began as responses to harsh economic times in the early 1980s are now being *cut* during another economic downturn a decade later. This raises unsettling questions about the perception of the role of S&T programs and ultimately the future of S&T in the states.

Given the dynamic nature and the range of success and failure among state S&T programs, what indicators can help to clarify the issues that state S&T programs will need to address in order to survive this uncertain decade? Finally, what does all this mean for current federal-state relations concerning S&T? Would increased federal support help the state S&T programs? Or would the support artificially perpetuate programs deserving to be terminated? What would the increased federal S&T efforts do to the balance of power between the states and Washington over policy questions? Could these hurdles be overcome to find an S&T policy arrangement acceptable to all parties?

Identifying the types of issues that are occurring in certain state programs can begin to suggest methods of study regarding state S&T survival or resurgence. At the least, understanding the scope of change in these programs will aid our knowledge of the current status of individual state S&T programs. Knowing this can help us determine the future concerns these programs will need to address in the remainder of the 1990s.

BACKGROUND

The 1980s marked the decade of growth for state S&T policy in the United States. Driven by economic hardships and federal cutbacks early in the Reagan administration, many state executives and legislators took the lead and created technology-based programs linking businesses, universities, and state governments to cultivate economic growth (Abelson 1986; Babbitt 1984).

In 1980, only 9 states had S&T agencies and offices. In three years that number had jumped to 22 states. By the end of the decade, at least 38 states had government organizations specifically designated for S&T missions, according to the National Governors' Association. By 1991, at least 45 states had S&T agencies to stimulate technological innovation (Atkinson 1988; Minnesota Department of Trade and Economic Development 1988). Their total budget exceeded $450 million per year and included over 250 separate programs (Atkinson 1991). State governors and legislatures established legislation providing legitimacy for these S&T efforts, further enhancing their credibility and sense of importance (Lambright and Rahm 1991).

The range of S&T programs developed in the 1980s was impressive. Most visible were the modern variations of the first "high technology" park—North Carolina's Research Triangle—established in the 1950s.

Tapping into the academic talent base in North Carolina, the state sought to keep that talent at home by developing a business park that focused on high technology industries. Developed as a response to the decline in North Carolina's agricultural and textile industries, the Research Triangle was a success that other states hoped to emulate (Rogers and Larsen 1984; National Governors' Association 1983).

In the first half of the 1980s, California's Silicon Valley and Massachusetts' Route 128 also showed to everyone the economic benefits associated with a university-based high tech state S&T/industrial development program. Various states, aware of their own relative strengths and weaknesses compared to these models of success, crafted S&T programs that fit their own needs and resources. Government-industry-university consortia; university-led "centers" designed to advance research with commercial potential; state incubator industry programs that provided capital, physical space, and talent to aid emerging technology-based companies were among some of the programs developed in the 1980s (Lambright and Rahm 1991).

In addition, the states also began to make more aggressive attempts to acquire major federal S&T projects. The securing of the Superconducting Super Collider (SSC) project by Texas—a multi-billion-dollar advanced particle physics research facility, through a package of cheap land, tax breaks, and substantial guaranteed state funding—was one example of the activist approach of the states in S&T (Walsh 1988; Lambright and Rahm 1991). New York's victory over California in acquiring the National Science Foundation's $5 million per year Earthquake Engineering Research Center was another example of state competition in the 1980s for what New York Governor Mario Cuomo called "high-tech pork" (Lambright and Rahm 1991; U.S. General Accounting Office 1987).

In effect, a new function of state government—S&T-based economic development—was emerging. This function took different forms in different places—either more basic scientific or more applied technological—depending upon the function's resources and legislative mandate. But the ultimate goal for everyone was the desire to use S&T for state economic success. And the federal government was beginning to initiate programs that would help at least some states achieve that goal.

THE FEDERAL GOVERNMENT'S ROLE

For the federal government, reaction was slow to this newly emerging policy arena. Although Washington has clearly been the dominant funder of U.S. science activities since World War II, federal aims and programs did not mesh neatly with those of state S&T agencies in the 1980s. The federal government's complex R&D funding mechanisms, mainly through "mission agencies," such as the Department of Defense, Department of Energy, and NASA, had traditionally been tailored toward providing goods applied to Washington needs. Second, federal support for basic research funds to universities through the National Institutes of Health and National Science Foundation related to aims of the scientific community (Rees 1987). Up to the 1980s, except possibly for agriculture, federal attention was away from the application of basic research funds and work at federally funded laboratories into economic development programs for the states.

With the states in the 1980s taking initiatives toward economic development, the federal government began adjustments to address this refocusing of policy. In Fiscal Year (FY) 1985, NSF expanded its EPSCoR (Experimental Program to Stimulate Competitive Research) program to help states with low levels of scientific research, and academic and industrial bases to more fully complement state S&T initiatives (NSF 1984). Begun in 1978 by NSF as a response to concerns over the geographic maldistribution of research awards, EPSCoR targeted five states with five-year grants to foster improvements in the S&T research environments in each state. In FY 1985, Congress increased the appropriations for EPSCoR, providing a larger base from which to help more states with underdeveloped S&T infrastructures. A third cycle of funding by the end of the 1980s targeted 17 different states for EPSCoR funding (NSF 1988).

Federal initiatives were also springing up within other agencies and departments. For example, as part of the Omnibus Trade and Competitiveness Act of 1988, the Department of Commerce created a Clearinghouse for State and Local Initiatives. The Clearinghouse was designed to be a data base on existing state S&T programs, which states could tap into for ideas in creating or improving their own programs.

From the perspectives of the Reagan and Bush administrations, these initiatives were substantial in ensuring that Washington would assist state S&T. However, critics were not as favorable. While it was clear that these programs had potential, they stood as symbols of the modest federal role. Critics found it anomalous that state governments were clearly in the lead on creating S&T economic competitiveness programs. In fact, as Commerce Undersecretary for Technology Robert M. White stated in announcing the Clearinghouse: "State and local governments are in the forefront of efforts to improve productivity, technology, and innovation" (U.S. Department of Commerce 1990).

Although the overall expenditures of states for this function were small in comparison to R&D expenditures of the federal government and industry, the states concentrated on areas of civilian R&D that were commercially important. It was the degree to which these state funds were targeted to economic development that made them stand out, and differentiated them from most federal R&D (Lambright 1991).

As the 1990s began, however, the state S&T agencies, offices, and programs started to become caught up in a new fiscal bind. Budget deficits of record proportion in many states gave rise to heated political battles and massive cuts in programs that were models for state S&T innovation, like those of Massachusetts and New York (Minerbrook 1991; Karmin 1991). Some of the S&T enterprises in these states did not survive. Others did, but questions remain as to how vigorous the survivors will be in the coming years.

To gather information on the current status of S&T in state government, informal telephone interviews were conducted with S&T agency officials in six key states. Respondents were asked about changes in budgets, programs, and personnel in their state S&T programs. Questions were posed on the political setting of their programs. In addition, we asked the officials to give what sense they had of events in other states active in S&T-based economic development. Second, officials from federal and other national organizations involved in S&T activities were interviewed on what was happening in the states and relevant situations at the federal level. The responses to this brief survey were compared to results from a 13-state comparative study of state S&T programs we prepared for NSF in the late 1980s (Lambright et al., 1989). Information from the earlier study and our "update" are discussed subsequently.

As with any study of state S&T programs, attempts to standardize data and make generalizations are difficult. States entered the S&T field at different times, limiting the ability to make comparisons. The sheer number and range of S&T programs also makes standardization difficult. Finally, gleaning information from state budgetary documents, which feature myriad separate agency-run S&T programs versus a more centralized state S&T program, prevents systematic study of some states and further highlights some of the obstacles to analyzing trends (Osborne 1988; Atkinson 1988; Lambright et al. 1989).

But what remained constant throughout the interviews to update the late 1980s study is that officials of prospering, struggling, or dying state S&T programs *all* agree that the 1990s constitute a time of turbulence for state S&T programs. This turbulence has taken different forms and had diverse consequences in various places, but some generalities emerge.

THE PROBLEMS AND THEIR IMPACT ON STATE S&T PROGRAMS

For the states, three separate factors have had the most negative impacts on state S&T programs in the past two years: (1) state budget crises, (2) political changes within states, and (3) programmatic shifts in policy focus. Although the impact has varied by state, the trends do suggest an overall decline in state S&T activities.

STATE BUDGET CRISES

The 1990s have seen an unprecedented number of state fiscal crises. States like Massachusetts, California, and New York suddenly incurred huge budget deficits during the first fiscal years in the 1990s. With 47 states showing decline in real personal income in 1990, the revenue coffers of almost all the states suffered. Budgeted programs had to be drastically reduced, if not cut altogether, if states were to balance their fiscal situations (Karmin 1991). Ohio, a state renowned for its innovative Thomas Edison Program, had to endure a state budget deficit between $350 million and $500 million (Berglund 1991; Karmin 1991). Illinois, another state with a substantial S&T program, ended up cutting $1.4 billion from a $26 billion budget to make ends meet (Strauss 1991). Big or small, most states have had to deal with fiscal problems of some magnitude in recent years.

In response, a number of state S&T programs began to fall on the budgetary chopping block. Preliminary figures announced at a meeting of the Science and Technology Council of States of the National Governors' Association showed that 11 out of 20 states decreased their S&T spending from FY 1991–92. Four states kept funding the same, and only five states increased funding (Layton 1991; Phelps 1991).[2]

Among the specific states that cut their programs were:

Illinois. This state's "fairly significant cuts" were among the most unsettling (Clark 1991). With the massive budget cuts and a change of administration in this state, S&T projects all but died in the past fiscal year. As an example, an Illinois official stated that the Technology Challenge Grant Program, the S&T program in Illinois with the best rate of success in the past two years, was heavily cut. In FY 1991 that program's budget was $17.2 million; in FY 1992 it was cut to $7.3 million, a drop of nearly 60 percent (Strauss 1991). Three other programs with multi-million-dollar budgets were cut back to zero. Personnel in the agency were cut by 20 percent, with some divisions losing 80 percent of their staff (Strauss, 1991).

Massachusetts. The Centers for Excellence Program was abandoned by the state (Clark 1991).

Michigan. Part of the Technology Deployment Service was cut as a state agency, only to be picked up again through the use of Michigan's Strategic Fund of oil and gas revenues (Clark 1991; Phelps 1991).

Pennsylvania. Funding for the Ben Franklin Partnership dropped nearly 20 percent in three years, from $31.5 million in FY 1988–89 to $25.4 million in FY 1991–92. Although personnel felt confident that the worst was behind them, the acceptance and even relief associated with a 20 percent cut highlight the storms afflicting state S&T. To survive is regarded as success in some cases (Cook 1991).

But, in keeping with the theme of turbulence, a few states had budgetary increases and expansions. In the survey described at the Science and Technology Council of States, it was noted that although 11 states slashed S&T funding and only 5 increased it, 10 states augmented personnel. This suggests they believed they had a long-term future. Among the examples of promising state activities mentioned were:

Louisiana. This state has reportedly just opened a state S&T office (Clark 1991).

Oklahoma and Montana. Both have increased and expanded the number of S&T programs (Clark 1991). Montana's primary S&T agency increased its administrative budget in the last legislative session. It was also given management authority for a $5.1 million R&D loan fund Murray 1991).

Arkansas. According to Annual Reports from the Arkansas Science and Technology Authority, basic research funding has increased from FY 1989–90, as has total seed capital investment funds (Arkansas 1989).

Of course, what helped these states is the fact that, for the most part, the current recession has spared most of their economies. Louisiana and Montana were among the top five states with the largest budget surpluses as a percentage of their state's budget in 1991 (Karmin 1991).

Other states have endured. New York, which survived a severe budget deficit that led to two protracted budget battles between the state legislature and Governor Mario Cuomo in 1989 and 1990, has kept its S&T programs alive. But officials inside Albany observe that "tremendous change," injurious to state S&T, occurred within the state and nationally since 1989 (Layton 1991).

Political Changes within States

Over 20 state houses, nearly half the nation, saw party turnover in the 1989–91 period (*Congressional Quarterly Almanac* 1988 and 1990; Layton 1991). Because of that, former officials who were S&T advocates were replaced by officials who, at the very least, did not have the same perspective as those who went before.[3]

In Tennessee, the new governor greatly diminished the role of S&T programs begun by his predecessor (Phelps 1991). In Ohio, the former Governor, Richard Celeste, who was a forceful advocate of state-sponsored S&T and helped set up the Thomas Edison Program, left under the term limit agreement for Ohio's chief executives (Phelps 1991). Illinois' new governor has helped lead the state legislature to make cuts in the state's S&T programs (Strauss 1991).

What is positive is that some S&T programs have now generated institutional support in the legislature, releasing them from the tenuous dependence on a state governor with whom they were closely associated. Montana's S&T agency, begun in 1985 by a Democratic governor, survived the gubernatorial turnover. It is for the most part "nonpartisan," according to an official with Montana's S&T program (Murray 1991). Although a new governor can be expected to react to difficult financial times by cutting programs his predecessor initiated, officials in states where S&T programs have survived have said that "strong bipartisan support" in the state legislature is the key factor responsible for their resilience. Ohio is a case in point (Phelps 1991). Presumably, state S&T programs that have shown clear "outputs" in technology transfer or successfully incubated new companies will be those with the greatest staying power.

Programmatic Shifts in Policy Focus

Some states, whose S&T programs have been less fiscally stressed, have nevertheless made policy shifts in their programs that will cause difficulties. These shifts can be positive in terms of finding the best fit between a program's goals and its state technological strengths. But the timing may cause programs to fail outright if the transition is not made carefully. In Minnesota, the state has refocused its S&T program more toward rural development through a quasi-private organization called Minnesota Private Inc. (Phelps 1991).

Other state S&T programs continue to try to exist in the private sector. Massachusetts, while having cut its state S&T programs, is maintaining some S&T activities through nonprofit and privatized organizations (Clark 1991). These programs may succeed. But S&T programs need long-term support to survive. In the private sector, these programs run a much greater risk of failure than as part of a state's budget. Certainly, the private sector will not support state S&T activities at the basic research end of the R&D continuum.

CONCLUSIONS

The 1990s are a difficult time for many state S&T programs. Budget problems and political changes have meant greater uncertainty for programs still relatively young. Created largely in the 1980s, they must sustain themselves in the 1990s.

It would seem that the needs of the states provide an opportunity for federal S&T programs to become a more critical ingredient of a state's S&T strategy. Certainly, states continue to seek to win the various federal competitions for centers and facilities. Also, states use their Washington representatives to write-in special appropriations for "earmarked" funding in their universities, often without benefit of peer review or other science-based reviews. Finally, the EPSCoR program and the DOC's Clearinghouse represent an important side of the states' federal environment.

These, however, are fragmented state-federal relations that involve positive and negative features. They reflect an absence of coordinated activity by the two governmental levels. They do not lead to a national effort linked to economic competitiveness. As a microcosm of the problem, Montana's new $5.1 million R&D loan fund is managed by its S&T agency. The federal EPSCoR grant is run out of Montana State University. Ideally, the federal and state funds would flow together through the same institution so as to bring about a greater critical mass of activity. But this cannot be assumed because of the competitive nature of the state fund activity and inevitable pressures within the state toward spreading the wealth (Murray 1991).

Whatever the case, given continued federal caution on the technology competitiveness front, states will probably, in the 1990s, largely continue to be on their own in charting a competitiveness strategy. They will do so in troubled seas. Hopefully, the more successful of these state "laboratories of democracy" will show the way for federal policy (Osborne 1988). Also, from here on, federal S&T policy and national S&T policy are not synonymous. A national policy must involve the states as well as Washington.

NOTES

1. This material is based in part upon work supported by the National Science Foundation under Grant Numbers SRS-8606984, SRS-8713477, and SRS-8907737.

2. The number of states is low because of lack of response by certain states and a lack of transferability of certain budget data into accurate trends of state S&T programs.

3. Sixteen governorships changed parties either through elections, party switches by a sitting governor, or with independents winning the office in 1990. Two state governors changed in 1989, three in 1988, and two governors have term limits that repeat in 1991.

REFERENCES

Abelson, Philip. 1986. Evolving state-university-industry relations. *Science* 240 (January): 265.

Arkansas. 1989. Arkansas S&T Authority annual report, FY 1990 and FY 1989.

Atkinson, Robert D. 1988. *State programs for technology development.* Report of the National Association of State Development Agencies, April.

————. 1991. Some states take the lead: Explaining reformation of state technology policies. *Economic Development Quarterly* 5 (February).

Babbitt, Bruce. 1984. The states and the reindustrialization of America. *Issues in Science and Technology* (Fall).

Berglund, Dan. 1991. Acting Director, Division of Technological Innovation, The Thomas Edison Program, Columbus, OH. Telephone interview, 2 October.

Clark, Marianne K. 1991. National Governors' Association, Washington, DC. Telephone interview, 25 September.

Congressional Quarterly Almanac. 1988 and 1990. CQ Inc.

Cook, William. 1991. Chief of Research Grants Division, Office of Technological Development, Harrisburg, PA. Telephone interview, 2 October.

Karmin, Monroe W. 1991. States under siege. *U.S. News and World Report,* 18 February: 44–46.

Lambright, W. Henry. 1991. *Science, technology, and the states: From the 1980s to the 1990s.* Paper presented at the AAAS, Science and Technology Policy Colloquium, Washington, DC, 11 and 12 April.

Lambright, W. Henry, Eva M. Price, and Albert H. Teich. 1989. *State science and technology indicators: An exploratory profile and analysis.* Report to the National Science Foundation, August. Grant No. SRS-8713477.

Lambright, W. Henry and Dianne Rahm. 1991. Science, technology, and the states. *Forum for Applied Research and Public Policy* 6 (3): 49–60.

Lambright, W. Henry, and Albert H. Teich. 1989. Science, technology, and state economic development. *Policy Studies Journal* 18 (Fall): 135–147.

Layton, Bruce. 1991. New York State Science and Technology Foundation, Albany. Telephone interview, 25 September.

Minerbrook, Scott. 1991. Wanted: Another, bigger miracle. *U.S. News and World Report,* 21 January: 58.

Minnesota Department of Trade and Economic Development. 1988. *State technology programs in the United States: 1988*. Report by the Office of Science and Technology, July.

Murray, Mary Ann. 1991. Finance Officer, Montana Science and Technology Alliance, Department of Commerce, Helena. Telephone interview, 20 November.

National Governors' Association. 1983. *Technology and growth: State initiatives in technology innovation*. Final Report of the Task Force on Technological Innovation, October.

National Science Foundation. 1984. Experimental Program to Stimulate Competitive Research (EPSCoR) Program Plan FY 1985 (November 19).

————. 1988. EPSCoR Science and Technology Action Plan FY 1989, draft report, 15 October.

Osborne, David. 1988. *Laboratories of democracy*. Boston: Harvard Business School Press.

Phelps, Paul B and Paul R. Brockman. 1992. *Science and technology programs in the states 1991*. Alexandria, VA: Advanced Development Distribution.

Rees, John. 1987. *State science policy and its implications for economic development: Towards an agenda for research*. Paper prepared for NSF workshop, Washington, DC, September.

Rogers, Everett M. and Judith K. Larsen. 1984. *Silicon Valley fever: Growth of high-technology culture*. New York: Basic Books.

Schmandt, Jurgen and Robert Wilson, eds. 1987. *Promoting high-technology industry: Initiatives and policies for state governments*. Boulder, CO: Westview Press.

Strauss, John. 1991. Manager, Office of Illinois Technology Advancement and Development, Chicago. Telephone interview, 2 October.

U.S. Department of Commerce. 1990. The Clearinghouse for State and Local Initiatives on Productivity, Technology, and Innovation. *U.S. Department of Commerce News*. Washington, DC: U.S. Department of Commerce.

U.S. General Accounting Office. 1987. *National Science Foundation: Problems found in decision process for awarding earthquake center*. Washington, DC: U.S. General Accounting Office. GAO/RCED087–146.

Walsh, John. 1988. Texas wins R&D center. *Science* 239: 248.

6 State Space Technology Programs: Boon to Competitiveness or Misdirected Efforts?

Arthur L. Levine

If all politics are local, as Tip O'Neill the famed former speaker of the United States House of Representatives said, then does it follow that U.S. competitiveness is rooted in the states and localities? If so, the impressive efforts of state and local governments in space technology should help make the United States competitive with Europe and Japan, the current and prospective leaders in space commerce. Whether these efforts bear fruit, however, depends on where they are directed and how they are managed.

Forty states are involved in space technology and related activities that have a bearing on U.S. competitiveness, as are many U.S. cities (Table 6.1). Twenty-four of these states have banded together in the Aerospace States Association (ASA) to help insure that the nation maintains its position in world-space commerce.

The prime motives for state and local space technology efforts are to attract new industry and increase chances that existing firms will tap into new space-related markets. But in looking after their own interests, states and localities are developing innovative approaches which can help build long-term U.S. competitiveness.

Opportunity for state and local entry into space technology stems from the growing prospects in "niche" markets. These include: (1) launch services for small satellites and suborbital flights (sounding rockets); (2) specialized satellite communications applications, such as mobile satellite services to facilitate personal worldwide telephone service and systems for locating trucks, emergency vehicles, and small boats; (3) earth monitoring for spotting environmental hazards, managing farm and forests, and

Table 6.1
States with Significant Space-Related Activites

STATES		ACTIVITIES
*ALABAMA	–	Three CCDS, University research, NASA Marshall Center, major space industries
*ALASKA	–	Operating spaceport (small launchers); university research; space development corporation planned
ARIZONA	–	University research; national telescope observatories; major space industries
*ARKANSAS	–	University research; space industry; plans to attract more
CALIFORNIA	–	California Space Institute (CALSPACE); university research; NASA Ames and JPL centers; Livermore lab; industry incentives and technical assistance; major space industries; teleports (Los Angeles, San Francisco)
*COLORADO	–	CCDS; University research; NOAA and NCAR labs; USAF academy; major space industries; teleport (Denver)
CONNECTICUT	–	University research; space industries; FCDS
*FLORIDA	–	Operational spaceport (small launchers); university research; NASA Kennedy center; USAF Cape Canaveral; industry incentives; major space industries; teleport (Miami)
GEORGIA	–	University research; major space industries; teleport (Atlanta)
*HAWAII	–	Spaceport planned (small and medium launchers); university research; national telescope observatories; teleport (Honolulu)
*IDAHO	–	University research
ILLINOIS	–	Illinois Space Institute; university research; Argonne and Fermi national labs; teleport (Chicago)
IOWA	–	University research; teleport (Des Moines)
KANSAS	–	University research
*KENTUCKY	–	University research; plans for attracting more space industry
*LOUISIANA	–	University research
*MAINE	–	University research; CCDS

Table 6.1 (continued)

STATES		ACTIVITIES
*MARYLAND	-	University research; NASA Goddard center; major space industries
*MASSACHUSETTS	-	University research; space industries; teleport (Boston)
MICHIGAN	-	CCDS; university research; major space firms; teleport (Detroit)
MINNESOTA	-	University research; space industries; teleport (Minneapolis, St. Paul)
*MISSISSIPPI	-	CCDS NASA Michoud; spaceport under study; university research
MISSOURI	-	University research; major space industries
*MONTANA	-	University research; plans to attract space industry
*NEBRASKA	-	University research
NEW JERSEY	-	University research; space industries
*NEW MEXICO	-	Spaceport under study; university research; Los Alamos National Lab; industry incentives planned; space industries
NEW YORK	-	CCDS; university research; NASA Goddard Institute for Space Studies; teleport (New York City)
NORTH CAROLINA	-	University research; space industries; teleport (Raleigh)
NORTH DAKOTA	-	University research
*OHIO	-	Two CCDSs; Ohio Aerospace Institute (OAI); university research; NASA Lewis center; USAF Wright Patterson; space industries; teleport (Columbus)
*OKLAHOMA	-	University research; space industries; teleport (Oklahoma City)
*PENNSYLVANIA	-	CCDS; university research; teleport (Pittsburgh)
*SOUTH DAKOTA	-	University research; NOAA remote sensing processing center
TENNESSEE	-	University research; USAF Tullahoma; space industries

Table 6.1 (continued)

STATES	ACTIVITIES
*TEXAS	– Two CCDS; University research; NASA Johnson center; state communications satellite under development; major space industries; teleports (Dallas – Ft. Worth; Houston)
*UTAH	– University research; space industries
*VIRGINIA	– University research; NASA Langley and Wallops centers; NASA Reston space station office; Pentagon; will launch small satellites from Florida spaceport and Wallops; major space industries
WASHINGTON	– University research; major space industries; teleport (Seattle)
*WISCONSIN	– CCDS; university research; teleport (Milwaukee)
DISTRICT OF COLUMBIA	– NASA headquarters; space industries; teleport (Washington, D.C.)

* = Member Aerospace States Association

Note: CCDS Stands for Centers for the Commercial Development of Space.

Sources: ASA; Space News; World Teleport Association; Personal interviews by author.

disaster relief; and (4) manufacturing of components, electronics, and fuel for rockets and satellites.

But many states and localities believe that they cannot sit back and wait for markets to develop. They are taking proactive stands by providing a wide range of incentives to existing or new space-related industries, such as direct investment, tax abatements, financing through earmarked bond issues, campaigns to attract venture capital and technical assistance, including help in developing low-cost manufacturing methods. Through ASA, whose members account for more than 250 congressional seats, states can work together to support commercial space policies favorable to both new and established space firms. Some states are seeking federal grants for space-related commercial facilities. In most states, the governor has championed state involvement, often designating the lieutenant-governor to supervise state efforts. While state economic development and agencies are often utilized, increasingly states are establishing public authorities to spearhead activities. State university systems have been in the lead in setting up space research programs, often in partnership with industry. But no single pattern has emerged, and in many states, agencies that should be working together seem to have unrelated agendas.

Can these efforts really succeed in bolstering U.S. space competitiveness? Are forces beyond the control of state and localities—such as major government subsidies of space industries in Europe, Japan, China, and the former Soviet Union and the opposition of the Bush administration to an industrial policy—dooming state efforts before they can mature? Are markets for space products and services strong enough to accommodate new U.S. ventures, given the lead of other nations and their ability to undercut U.S. firms through subsidized pricing?

TYPES OF SPACE TECHNOLOGY PROGRAMS

State and local space technology programs fall into four main categories: spaceports, teleports, space research with commercial applications, and incentives to attract and retain space-related industries.

Spaceports are facilities for launching commercial spacecraft and may also be utilized as landing sites for reentering space vehicles. Payload processing and other satellite and launch services are done at spaceports. Florida has a spaceport with launches planned from its Cape San Blas site. Alaska plans to convert a site used for launching small scientific payloads to commercial use. Hawaii has an active spaceport development program. New Mexico and Mississippi are studying the feasibility of setting-up state launch facilities.

Teleports are facilities for sending and receiving satellite communications worldwide, as well as other transmissions, notably through local and regional area network fiber optic ground links. Teleports, located in over 20 U.S. cities (see Table 6.1), are usually associated with a commercial real estate venture or other economic development and generally offer value-added telecommunications services, such as providing special feeds to cable companies, private networks, and other tailored services. In some cases, local governments are partners in teleports. But in all cases, local governments play a pivotal role in providing infrastructure and services needed for teleport operations.

Space technology research programs with commercial applications generally involve universities as the main center of activity. Industrial firms and federal laboratories are usually participants. States may also support commercially focused research by affiliating with one or more of the 17 NASA-sponsored Centers for the Commercial Development of Space (CCDS) (see Table 6.2). States receive support for research programs through the NASA Space Grant College program.[1]

Incentive programs have grown both in scope and intensity in the last few years as competition for obtaining new industries and holding on to existing firms has heightened due to the recession.

SPECIFIC PROGRAMS

Spaceports

Building a major spaceport for large- and medium-sized launch vehicles (capable of lifting up to 15,000 pounds to geosynchronous orbit) is expensive, requiring hundreds of millions of dollars and $10 million or more in yearly operating expenses. Currently, there is sufficient capacity in existing launch facilities to accommodate commercial launches of 40 medium and large launch vehicles per year. Estimates indicate, however, that only between 15 and 20 commercial launches a year in these classes will be needed for the next decade. Up to 60 launches per year may be needed for small launch vehicles, which send up sounding rockets, microsats (weighing under 300 pounds), and lightsats (under 2,000 pounds). These smaller payloads, however, can be lifted by larger rockets when they ride "piggyback" along with heavier satellites (Corcoran and Beardsley 1990; de Selding 1991). In addition, the Pegasus winged rocket designed to be launched from an airplane has been successfully tested by its developers, Orbital Sciences Corporation and Hercules Aerospace

Table 6.2
Centers for the Commercial Development of Space

Materials Processing
Center for Advanced Materials, Battelle Columbus Laboratories,
   Columbus, Ohio
Center for Development of Commercial Crystal Growth in Space,
   Center for Advanced Materials Processing, Clarkson
   University, Potsdam, New York
Consortium for Materials Development, University of Alabama-
   Huntsville, Huntsville, Alabama
Center for Space Vacuum Epitaxy, University of Houston, Houston,
   Texas

Life Science
Center for Macromolecular Cystallography, University of Alabama-
   Birmingham, Birmingham, Alabama
Center for Cell Research, Pennsylvania State University,
   University Park, Pennsylvania
Center for Bioserve Space Technologies, University of Colorado,
   Boulder, Colorado

Remote Sensing
Center for Mapping, Ohio State University, Columbus, Ohio
ITD Space Remote Sensing Center, National Space Technology
   Laboratories, Mississippi

Automation and Robotics
Center for Space Automation & Robotics, University of Wisconsin,
   Madison, Wisconsin
Center for the Commercial Development of Autonomous and Man-
   Controlled Robotic Sensing Systems of Space, Environmental
   Research Institute of Michigan, Ann Arbor, Michigan

Space Propulsion
Center for Advanced Space Propulsion, University of Tennessee
   Space Institute, Tullahoma, Tennessee

Space Structures and Materials
Center on Materials for Space Structures, Case Western Reserve
   University, Cleveland, Ohio

Space Power
Center for Commercial Development of Space Power, Texas A&M
   Research Foundation, College Station, Texas
Center for Commercial Development of Space Power, Auburn
   University, Auburn, Alabama

Advanced Satellite Communications:
*Florida Atlantic University, Boca Raton, Florida
*University of Maryland, College Park, Maryland

* = Established 1991; Other CCDS were established from 1985 to 1987.

Source: National Aeronautics and Space Administration.

Table 6.3
Competition in Launch Sites

UNITED STATES	Cape Canaveral Air Force Station, Florida
	Kennedy Space Center, Florida
	Florida Spaceport (Cape San Blas)
	Vandenberg Air Force Base, California
	Wallops Island, Virginia
	Alaska (Poker Flats)
	Hawaii (two sites under study)
	New Mexico (under study)
	Mississippi (under study)
SOVIET UNION	Tyuratam
	Kapustin Yar
	Plesetsk
ESA/FRANCE	Guiana Space Center, French Guiana
JAPAN	Tanegashima
	Kagoshima Space Center
	Uchi Noura
	Hokkaido Space Center (under study)
CHINA	Shuang-cheng tzu, Gansu Provice
	Xichang, Sichuan Province
	Jiuquan, west of Beijing
	Hainan (under study)
ITALY	San Marcos (off coast of Kenya)
AUSTRALIA	Cape York (under study)
INDIA	Sriharikota
SWEDEN	Kiruna

Company. Mobile launchers, carried on trucks and capable of lifting satellites weighing 350 pounds, are also being developed.

There is fierce competition for launch business. More than half of all launches will be carried out from outside the United States, mainly by Arianespace, a European firm, from its pad in French Guiana, but also from other foreign sites (see Table 6.3). Launch prices offered by Arianespace, as well as Chinese and Soviet firms, are up to 30 percent lower than prices of U.S. firms for comparable services. Competition from fiber optics has reduced prospects for communications satellites, which make up a large part of commercial launches, and technological improvements promise to lengthen the life of medium and large size Comsats from an average of 10 to 14 years (Pelton 1990; de Selding 1991). These developments will further reduce demand for commercial launches. Moreover, the U.S. Air Force makes available its facilities at Cape Canaveral (Florida) for commercial launches and offers technical assistance. There is enough capacity for launching *all* planned commercial large, medium, and small satellites in existing U.S. government and Arianespace facilities.

In recognition of these facts, states have modified their spaceport plans to aim more at the market for small launchers. The Florida Spaceport Authority had originally planned to rebuild three unused U.S. Air Force pads at Cape Canaveral for small and medium-sized launch vehicles. The limited market and difficulty in attracting venture capital caused a change in plans. Now the authority is concentrating on the small satellite and sounding rocket markets. The Cape San Blas facility, a launching site at Elgin Air Force base refurbished by the authority, is suited to launches of sounding rockets. The authority plans to launch small satellites from Canaveral by refurbishing one former Air Force launch pad.

The Florida spaceport's first launch, however, came from a mobile launcher in Mexico, which lifted a suborbital payload to study the solar extended corona during the total eclipse of the sun on July 11, 1991.

The Florida authority is also working to improve prospects for U.S. firms that launch medium and large vehicles from Air Force facilities at Canaveral, where both military and commercial launches are accommodated. The control center and launch preparation facilities at the Air Force pads are out of date and need improvement. The authority is seeking a Department of Transportation Grant to refurbish them. This would increase efficiency and lower launch costs, helping U.S. firms to compete with foreign rivals. The role of the Florida Spaceport Authority has also broadened to support research efforts and to attract new industry in joint programs with the Florida Technology Research and Development Authority (see later sections in this chapter on space research and industry incentives).

The Hawaii Space Development Authority is pushing ahead to build a spaceport for small and medium launchers on one of two sites on the Big Island of Hawaii. It is likely that the spaceport will concentrate, at least initially, on the small and sounding rocket classes. The state expects to spend $5 to $8 million for access roads, water, sewer, electricity, and communications for either of the two sites. The state does not plan to play a direct role in financing or building the spaceport, rather counting on an international consortium led by Japanese business firms that have shown interest in the project. No plans to issue state bonds or other state financial support have been made (Flagg 1991). Environmentalists and local residents near the prospective sites have vigorously opposed the spaceport.

Eleven private firms have expressed interest in launching sounding rockets from a firing range owned and operated by the University of Alaska at Fairbanks. The launching site at Poker Flats offers proximity to the North Pole (an advantage for launching into polar orbits) and a 90 percent rate of success for recent suborbital launches by universities. Another advantage is that the Alaska site is not involved with a military installation, which requires that a host of government regulations be satisfied before a launch can be made. The Alaska site will also benefit from a $30 million federal grant to finance new roads, water and sewer systems, and better optics and communications systems (*Florida Today* 1991). Firms have also expressed interest in launching small satellites from Poker Flats. This would require upgrading of launching facilities that are now capable of sounding rocket launches only.

Teleports

The boom in the worldwide telecommunications business is expected to continue for the next several years, making prospects for teleports good. Teleports, unlike spaceports, do not rely exclusively on space technology for their success. State or local involvement in teleports enhances prospects for success by providing favorable conditions for obtaining zoning approvals, permits to lay fiber optic cables, tax abatements, and support services.

Teleports contribute to competitiveness by making available to U.S. firms a wide choice of telecommunications options providing versatile interconnectivity to local, regional, and international markets. A recent report by the U.S. National Telecommunications and Information Administration found that international teleports are essential for the expansion of U.S. international information trade. Teleports also stimulate regional economic development through their partnerships with commercial office parks and other development initiatives. The Bay Area (San Francisco) and the New York City Teleport are also working in partnership with regional transportation authorities to upgrade road, rail, and ship-handling capacity. The aim is to attract business by offering an integrated telecommunications and transportation infrastructure, similar to a successful development in Osaka, Japan, including international air, sea, and information "ports" (Reiser 1990).

The New York City Teleport, in operation since 1985, is a partnership of The Port Authority of New York and New Jersey, the City of New York, and Merrill Lynch. The teleport has 17 satellite earth stations for domestic and international communications and regional fiber optic hookups serving Manhattan, Brooklyn, Queens, New Jersey, and Staten Island. The teleport includes a real estate development with more than 700,000 square feet of space of which 160,000 was developed by a consortium of Japanese firms. Customers of the teleport include financial services firms, telecommunications companies, and major broadcast and cable networks (Levine 1989).

The Atlanta Teleport, owned and operated by Crawford Communications, is a stand-alone variety without an associated office park. Yet it provides a host of services to regional telecommunications and industrial firms that enhance their ability to be internationally competitive (Schuster 1991).

Teleports face increasing competition from ground-based cellular and worldwide mobile satellite systems as well as from universities and firms who sell unused time on their satellite uplinks (Boeke 1991). This will require teleport operators to increase their range of offerings, tailor their services more to specific customer needs, and reduce costs to compensate for lower profit margins. Local governments can help by shaping policies that facilitate low-cost versatile teleport operations.

Space Research Programs

Topics include: (1) automation and robotics; (2) materials processing under microgravity conditions with applications for improved pharmaceuticals and high-strength materials; (3) biomedical studies for long duration space flight with many applications to earth-bound medicine; (4) remote sensing for earth monitoring of environmental hazards, agriculture, mining and oil exploration, and mapping; (5) spacepropulsion; (6) space power; (7) superconductivity; and (8) specialized computing and electronics applications. Many of these topics match the list of "critical technologies" in which the United States is losing ground to other nations, according to a 1991 report of the Council on Competitiveness.[2]

State research programs also emphasize increasing the capacity of a state and its region in basic technological knowledge by awarding graduate and undergraduate fellowships. Many also conduct outreach projects to interest elementary and high school students, minorities, and women in math and science education. Increasingly, international participation in research programs is being encouraged by inviting foreign companies and students to participate.

Some states have established formal space research institutes. Others coordinate activities of universities, federal laboratories, and industry through university-led consortia.

The California Space Institute (CALSPACE), based at the University of California (U.C.) San Diego, established in 1980, was the first state-space institute. It supports in-house research in remote sensing and solar system science and also administers a grant program of approximately

$600,000 annually to fund investigators at the nine U.C. campuses. Research in robotics, expert systems, and remote sensing for forestry and agriculture applications is especially geared to commercialization. In 1990, Dr. Sally Ride, a former astronaut who led a study on long-range space plans and served on the National Commission on Space, was named CALSPACE director. This appointment is expected to give new impetus to the state's space research efforts. Recently, CALSPACE officials have broadened views on what is needed, beyond academic research, to spur commercial space development by emphasizing the importance of state and local governments working with colleges and private industry (Polsky 1991).

The Ohio Aerospace Institute (OAI) got under way in 1989 with a $500,000 line item in the Ohio Board of Regents budget and enjoys substantial support from NASA. OAI is a consortium of nine Ohio universities, the NASA Lewis Research Center, and the U.S. Air Force Wright Patterson Base in Dayton, plus more than a dozen industrial firms. Housed in temporary quarters near the Lewis Center, it will move in 1993 to a state funded $10.6 million permanent home on the Lewis grounds and will also maintain a branch at Wright Patterson. An act of Congress gave NASA permission to lease land at Lewis to the Institute at no cost and to provide major technical assistance and personnel services, as well as time on its Cray supercomputer (U.S. Congress 1988). OAI's missions are to build a regional capability in aerospace and to create an atmosphere of mutual trust in which industry and university people can work together, thus displacing the prevalent feeling among industry executives that university researchers are too far removed from practical considerations to provide much help to improving products and services.[3] This is done in joint research projects and special "focus groups" in which university, industry, and government personnel identify key areas for investigation (Salkind 1991). Such face-to-face encounters are considered the best mechanism to improve prospects for commercialization of academic research findings (Osborne 1990).

The Illinois Space Institute has a grant program of approximately $700,000 to fund investigators at four universities in the state, both public and private. Sources of funding include the NASA Space Grant College Program and matching contributions from industry and the state government. Emphasis is on encouraging more students to major in aerospace engineering, astrophysics, and spacecraft design to better position the state to compete for NASA and commercial contracts (Solomon 1991).

The Florida Technological Research and Development Authority (TRDA) awards most of its grants for space-related investigations. In

1990, these amounted to $600,000 to six Florida universities. TRDA works in conjunction with the Florida Spaceport Authority to develop a research agenda. TRDA receives 25 percent of the revenues generated from the sale of Challenger auto license plates, which commemorates astronauts killed in the 1986 shuttle explosion. This source brings in about $1 million annually. In addition, the Florida Department of Education provided $600,000 in 1990. TRDA has cooperative programs with the Virginia Center for Innovative Technology and is working with Colorado, Alabama, California, and Canada to establish joint projects. The collaboration with Virginia will result in the launch from the Florida Spaceport facility at Cape San Blas of a small remote sensing satellite to study environmental and atmospheric conditions in Southern Florida. TRDA also funds four upcoming launches from Cape San Blas of Florida University experiments. A noteworthy initiative is the Direct Readout Project to be carried out in cooperation with the National Oceanic and Atmospheric Administration (NOAA) in which teachers and students will get training in how to receive satellite signals and read and interpret satellite data (Kinney 1991).

Virginia conducts a vigorous space research effort in close cooperation with the NASA Langley Research Center located in Hampton, Virginia, and the NASA Goddard Space Flight Center in nearby Maryland. Space research is promoted by the Virginia Center for Innovative Technology (CIT) which has a division for space industry development. The VASTAR satellite program is a joint venture between CIT and Orbital Sciences Corporation to validate and demonstrate the capabilities of the firm's planned systems of 23 lightsats for data relay (Morgan 1991).

The NASA CCDS are consortia of industry, universities, and government. Centers are located at both state and private institutions. NASA selected applicants for grant awards partly on the basis of pledges of funds or in-kind contributions by industrial firms, state governments, universities, and federal laboratories. States can participate in any CCDS, including those located in another state. The State of Florida, for example, is an affiliate of a center in New York. Three states—New York, Texas, and Wisconsin—provide substantial funds to one or more CCDS. Research agendas of CCDS are largely industry-driven. NASA provides funding of approximately $1 million per year to each CCDS, as well as technical expertise and free flights on the space shuttle and expendable launchers for some CCDS experimenters. When a research project is funded by an industrial affiliate, the firm generally has first refusal rights for patents or patent licenses for products or processes developed from the project (Levine 1989).

The slow pace of industry investment in CCDSs has been criticized by some members of Congress, particularly Senator Barbara Mikulski (D-MD) who requested the General Accounting Office to review the program. GAO called for a phasing out of federal subsidies for the program unless industry steps up its funding rapidly. To spur centers to become self-sufficient, GAO urged NASA to establish goals for each center and to evaluate progress periodically. Corrective measures should be taken for lagging centers. If they do not work, termination of NASA support is recommended. GAO also advised NASA to improve its programs for CCDS fiscal management and for selection of payloads for space flight experiments proposed by CCDS investigators (U.S. General Accounting Office 1991).

Under the original CCDS concept, the centers were expected to garner enough industry support so that the federal funds would end after five to seven years. Most centers opened from 1985 to 1987. The shuttle accident of 1986 deprived the centers of flight opportunities to conduct space-based research for three years, damaging their ability to attract the participation of nonaerospace companies. As a result, NASA relaxed its time demands for self-sufficiency. The diminishing near-term market prospects for pharmaceuticals and other products made in microgravity has also hurt industry funding interest (Vilamill 1991). NASA has been pressuring centers with poor industry funding records to restructure, threatening funds cutoff if industry grants were not forthcoming (Lawler and Marcus 1991).

A casualty of these trends was the former CCDS at Vanderbilt University in Nashville, Tennessee, which conducted research for space processing of engineering materials. Established in 1986, the center initially had 12 industry affiliates but this number dwindled to three by 1991. While industry affiliates provided in-kind contributions to Vanderbilt, no cash was forthcoming. NASA and Vanderbilt agreed to close the center in October 1991 (Saunders 1991; U.S. General Accounting Office 1991).

Some CCDSs have attracted increasing industry support, although none are expected by become self-sufficient before 1995 (U.S. General Accounting Office 1991). NASA wants to continue funding of all CCDSs for several more years beyond 1991, believing that this will permit the agency to better shape the course of U.S. commercial space activities. "I don't want the [centers] to run off in five years and become totally self-sufficient," said James Rose, NASA's assistant administrator for commercial programs. "Their ability [to do] anything useful to stimulate commercial space may go away" (Lawler and Marcus 1991, 1).

The stimulus of research aimed at space-based advancements can also lead to improvements in ground-based processes. Crystal growth experiments for microgravity conditions led several firms to adopt new methods for earth-based investigations. This work, performed at the CCDS at the University of Alabama, Birmingham, in conjunction with Georgia Institute of Technology, an affiliate of the Birmingham Center, is illustrative of research that would not have been carried out for ground based activity (Suddath 1991).

Incentives

Increasingly, states and localities are offering incentives to attract and retain space-related industries. Florida offers sales and use tax exemption to all commercial launch vehicles, their payloads, and associated fuels. In addition, Florida has reserved $100 million in bonds to finance space ventures. The bonds would be backed by the companies, but interest is exempt from state taxes and may be federal tax exempt if legislation goes through Congress to treat spaceports like airports (Ellegood 1991).

California is offering an array of incentives and technical assistance to keep existing aerospace firms that employ over 200,000 persons in the state, as well as to attract new space-related enterprise. During the first half of 1991, the state spent $17 million to start the California Supplier Improvement Program, which offers community college instruction tailored to each firm. The program seeks ways to reduce costs while improving quality. A Business Environmental Assistance Center eases industry concerns and helps firms comply with state environmental regulations. The California commerce department, working with the City of Torrance, successfully thwarted a move by the Hughes Aircraft Electronic Dynamics Division to an out-of-state location. With the cooperation of the local power company, unions, and community colleges, a package of state-sponsored education and training programs for company employees and financial incentives for energy conservation was arranged (Polsky 1991).

New York City invested $12 million to build roads, sewers, and water lines serving the teleport area. The land on which the teleport stands is owned by the city and leased for 40 years to the Port Authority for real estate operations. The city granted real estate tax abatements to initial tenants who pay no taxes for the first 13 years and only partial taxes for the next 10. The city receives 8 percent of gross revenues from real estate operations and 25 percent of profits from Teleport Communications, a subsidiary of Merrill Lynch, after the private firm has received a 21 percent return (Levine 1989).

MARKET OUTLOOK

State space technology programs should take the outlook for space markets into careful account before committing resources to specific programs. States that have conducted strategic audits of their economies and have probed the competitive capabilities of their resident industries tend to have the best economic development systems (Osborne 1990). If a state finds that it is using resources to back an initiative for which another state would have a better chance at success, it should defer or initiate a cooperative program. One of the strengths of ASA is that it facilitates information sharing and deters unproductive competition among states.

Except for business related to communications satellites and associated ground equipment, U.S. firms are not expected to make profits in any commercial space ventures until the late 1990s.

Spaceports that depend on repeat launch business face limited markets. The U.S. remote sensing industry, estimated at $125 million in 1991, is small but growing; worldwide the market is dominated by the French firm Spot Image, and the Japanese are expected to enter it soon. The outlook for space-based products made in microgravity is that many years of major investment are still needed.

To some degree, states have already modified their space technology plans based on market outlook. Florida is concentrating on launching small satellites and sounding rockets from its spaceport and is attempting to help make commercial launches of medium and large satellites from Air Force launch pads more competitive. It is also integrating spaceport operations with space research and ground facilities. California, Ohio, and Virginia are emphasizing research in areas such as automation and robotics, remote sensing and ground equipment for satellite systems, in which growing commercialization is likely.

FEDERAL POLICY

Critics of federal commercial space policy have long contended that it is long on rhetoric but short on specific measures to help fledgling space firms (Levine 1989). New space firms have found it especially difficult to satisfy a maze of launch, radio frequency, environmental, and export license regulations enforced by several agencies before they can loft spacecraft or conduct space operations. The Reagan administration was firmly opposed to direct cash subsidies to space firms as part of its anathema to an industrial policy. Although the Bush administration has continued on this course, it has also taken steps to ease the regulatory burden and to provide more indirect help. A federal commercial space policy, released in February 1991, provides guidelines calling for agencies to use commercial space products "to the fullest extent feasible" and to weigh government overhead and labor costs fully when determining whether to carry out a service or make a product in-house or through a contract (National Space Council 1991). Space commerce advocates have claimed that some agencies tilt the balance in favor of in-house work through accounting practices that undercharge hard-to-calculate government costs. Another important change is to ease rules allowing agencies to pay termination costs to companies whose contracts have been canceled due to budget cuts or other reasons after the company has put in considerable work. Previously, the Office of Management and Budget (OMB) had to decide whether to approve termination liability on a case-by-case basis (Lawler 1991). This change has already given a boost to the Florida incentive program. Florida agreed to issue bonds on behalf of Spacehab, Inc., a firm that makes a module for conduct of experiments that fits into the space shuttle bay. Under the bond arrangement, Spacehab had to pledge to pay the principal and interest on the bonds. Among the conditions Florida imposed on the company was that its contract with NASA have a termination liability clause (Ellegood 1991).

The administration is also encouraging agencies to be "anchor tenants" for company R&D projects through issuance of long-term, sole-source contracts. This arrangement provides a stream of income to the firm, permitting development of the product or service until it is ready for wider sales to government or commercial customers. The Defense Advanced Research Projects Agency of the Department of Defense is an anchor tenant for Orbital Sciences's Pegasus launcher. NASA is an anchor tenant for Spacehab. These developments should provide a more stable atmosphere for commercial ventures, while permitting the federal government to be flexible in specific cases.

Yet the total amount of indirect federal help (under $400 million annually) committed to the commercial space industry pales before the billions of direct aid provided by foreign governments to their space firms. Commercial space advocates would like to see a national program for space industrial competitiveness backed by much greater financial support. The financial community, although encouraged by recent administration actions, feels that the financial support is not substantial enough. As Paul Nisbet, of Prudential Securities, put it: "The government probably won't have an effect until it subsidizes programs to put American companies on an equal basis with the Europeans, Japanese, and Soviets" (Lawler 1991).

CONCLUSION

Of the four types of space technology efforts by states and localities, research programs are likely to contribute most to U.S. competitiveness. Such programs target many critical technologies in which the United States is losing ground to foreign nations. Increasingly, industry is a full participant in these programs, and where they have not been active enough, as in the case of some CCDSs, remedial steps are being taken. It would be helpful if more emphasis could be placed on applied research, which can lead to penetrating niche markets and to developing value-added features for advanced systems.[4]

Given the extent of competition and the high costs involved, state investments in major spaceports should be approached with great caution. If a state can convert an existing site and concentrate on small launchers, a contribution to U.S. competitiveness may result. If the spaceport also facilitates launches of scientific payloads of investigators in state research programs, the benefits will increase. Teleports contribute to U.S. competitiveness through upgrading U.S. international information trade and stimulating regional development. Incentives to space industries are called for in some cases, but they can be costly in lost revenue and may not be useful if the industry is not viable due to market conditions, lack of suitable labor pools, or other problems.

States and local governments can maximize their efforts through better management and integration. Activities in each of the four categories of state efforts can reinforce one another through better coordination. State science and technology agencies, economic development agencies, and universities often do not mesh their space-related activities let alone coordinate them with other high technology programs.[5] This lack of integration occurs in nonspace technology programs in the states as well (Lambright and Teich 1989).

Through ASA, governors are taking a greater interest in space technology programs in their states. (Only a representative appointed by the governor can serve as a delegate to ASA.) The interest of chief executives should help in integration efforts, which often can be best handled by state S&T agencies. These agencies are in a good position to coordinate specific aspects of space technology research (such as in biomedicine, electronics, and automation) with similar research in other state and local technology programs.

Making the United States more competitive will also require dealing head on with lower prices offered by foreign firms as well as overcoming their lead in launchers and value-added products. States' efforts, particularly as they are focused through ASA, can serve as catalysts to bring about changes in federal policy to provide targeted assistance to research programs and firms likely to develop competitive products and services.

State space technology activities have strong potential to contribute significantly to U.S. competitiveness. But this can only be accomplished if states and localities develop strategic plans, integrate their space technology activities with other technology initiatives, and work effectively to move the national government toward a more realistic commercial space policy.

NOTES

1. Forty-six states and the District of Columbia are recipients of these grants, which are usually awarded to consortia of universities. Grants may be used for research, curriculum development, and fellowships. A maximum of $325,000 per year for five years may be awarded. Kentucky, Nebraska, Vermont, and Wyoming are not recipients but are considering applying (Dash 1991).

2. According to the Council on Competitiveness (1991), the United States is weak or losing ground badly in aspects of materials processing, leading edge scientific instruments, design for manufacturing, integrated circuit fabrications and testing equipment, automation and robotics, electronic components (such as actuators, laser devices) electroluminescent displays and optical information storage, and high fuel economic/power density engines.

3. Studies indicate that business is generally dissatisfied with the management and results of state-supported university-industry research centers in nonspace technology (Osborne 1990).

4. An example of a value-added development occurred when U.S. firms modified a military device for receiving signals from the Pentagon's Navstar Positioning Satellite System. The commercial device, popular with small boat users, calculates latitude and longitude and weighs under three pounds—in contrast to the 17-pound military version. It is also much cheaper. When the Defense Department needed thousands of receivers in the Saudi Desert during the Gulf War, it turned to commercial suppliers, since their devices were readily available and less costly, even though not as precise (Pollack 1991).

5. This statement is based on interviews by the author with state officials and academic observers in California, Florida, Georgia, New York, Ohio, and Virginia, as well as discussions with federal officials.

REFERENCES

Boeke, Cynthia L. 1991. Teleports in transition: Strategies to survive in the 1990s. *Via Satellite* (August): 20–28.

Corcoran, Elizabeth and Tim Beardsley. 1990. The new space race. *Scientific American* (July): 73–84.

Council on Competitiveness. 1991. *Gaining new ground: Technology priorities for America's future.* Washington, DC: Council on Competitiveness.

Dash, Julius. 1991. Director, NASA Office of University Programs, Washington, DC. Telephone interview, 10 July.

de Selding, Peter B. 1991. Arianespace foresees slower launch market in late '90s. *Space News*, 11–17 March, 16.

Ellegood, Edward. 1991. Florida Stateport Authority. Telephone interview, 27 June.

Flagg, Richard. 1991. Project Manager, Hawaii Spaceport, Honolulu. Telephone interview, 1 July.

Florida Today. 1991. Alaska launches bid for space business. *Florida Today,* 5 May, 10E.

Kinney, Frank. 1991. Director, Florida Technological Research and Development Authority, Melbourne. Telephone interview, 17 May.

Lambright, W. Henry and Albert Teich. 1989. Science, technology, and state economic development. *Policy Studies Journal* 18 (Fall): 135–147.

Lawler, Andrew. 1991. Bush bolsters commercial space. *Space News*, 18–24 February, 20.

———— and Daniel J. Marcus. 1991. NASA encouraged to make centers self-sufficient. *Space News*, 8–14 April, 1.

Levine, Arthur. 1989. Space technology and state competitiveness. *Policy Studies Journal* 18 (Fall): 148–163.

Morgan, Steve. 1991. Director of Space Industries, Virginia Center for Innovative Technology, Herndon. Telephone interview, 16 April.

National Space Council. 1991. *U.S. commercial space policy guidelines.* Washington, DC: National Space Council.

Osborne, David. 1990. Refining state technology programs. *Issues in Science and Technology* (Summer): 55–61.

Pelton, Joseph. 1990. New transmissions technologies: satellites and fiber optics in the 1990s. *Via Satellite* (September): 20–26.

Pollack, Andrew. 1991. In U.S. technology, a gap between arms and VCR's. *New York Times*, 4 March, 8D.

Polsky, Debra. 1991. California seeks to keep space firms from straying. *Space News*, 11–17 February, 8.

Reiser, John J., Jr. 1990. The teleport: 21st century information ports. *Via Satellite* (August): 20–23.

Salkind, Michael. 1991. President, Ohio Aerospace Institute, Brookpark. Personal interview, 18 March.

Saunders, Renne. 1991. Vanderbilt U. first causality of CCDS effort. *Space News*, 16–22 September, 1 and 20.

Schuster, James. 1991. Manager, Atlanta Teleport, Crawford Satellite Services. Personal interview, 24 June.

Solomon, Wayne. 1991. University of Illinois at Urbana and Chair, Illinois University Space Consortium. Telephone interview, 18 July.

Suddath, Fred. 1991. Director, Information Technology Center, Georgia Institute of Technology, Atlanta. Telephone interview, 24 June.

U.S. Congress. 1988. National Aeronautics and Space Capital Development Program Act. Public Law 100–685. Washington, DC: U.S. Government Printing Office.

U.S. General Accounting Office. 1991. *Commercial use of space: Many grantees making progress, but NASA oversight should be improved.* Washington, DC: U.S. General Accounting Office. Report No. GAO NSIAD 91–42.

Vilamill, Ana M. 1991. NASA Office of Commercial Programs, Washington, DC. Personal interview, 4 April.

7 Basic Research in the States

Linda E. Parker

Since the 1950s, public support of basic scientific research has been undertaken primarily by the federal government for long-term economic and societal needs, as well as for its own needs (e.g., defense). Within the last few years, a growing number of states have become aware of the benefits of including basic research sponsorship in their science and technology initiatives, which are supported for direct economic benefit to the state. As a result, the number of programs that include basic research components has increased rapidly. Confusion is mounting concerning how to examine the impact of the programs. Models for conducting impact studies of state-level basic research programs are in their infancy, yet state legislators must vote on future spending for the programs guided by whatever information is available to them. This chapter examines why confusion exists and how to begin to think about this type of program evaluation.[1]

RATIONALE

Three goals underlie federal and state support of basic research:

- The intrinsic intellectual value of extending knowledge in scientific and engineering fields
- The accomplishment of a specific government mission, such as improving public health or the environment
- The enhancement of economic competitiveness (Bloch 1986).

While these goals are common to both levels of government, they differ in levels of importance. The federal government has traditionally funded basic research to expand scientific knowledge and understanding for its own use. For states, this is not a dominant rationale. More focused economic and workforce needs cause state policymakers to support basic research in order to address specific governmental missions and enhance economic competitiveness.

The goal of accomplishing specific governmental missions reflects the role that basic research plays in making it possible for governments to ensure the well-being of their inhabitants and resources. For example, improving the quality of water in a particular region may involve basic research to identify specific pollutants that have not been discovered previously. This goal is also more prominent in federal than state programs.

The third goal acknowledges the contributions of basic research to states' economic competitiveness. Basic research discoveries often underlie technological advances in many important areas, leading to advanced products, automated production systems, competitive pricing, and increased productivity. Improving performance through research enhances competitive position (National Science Foundation 1991). This goal predominates at the state level.

The premise behind state R&D programs in general is that knowledge and technology contribute to a state's economic vitality by "assisting existing business, developing employment opportunities, creating new businesses, and attracting the branches and headquarters of out-of-state firms. Universities . . . play a key role both because they provide specific services and because a good university system is considered a general attraction to firms" (Research and Policy Committee 1986, 46). State sponsorship of basic research supports knowledge generation and the training of future scientists and engineers. This two-for-one deal is particularly attractive because it involves an active research environment for businesses and students simultaneously, which contributes to the creation of more job opportunities within a state for graduates of its science and engineering programs. By keeping graduates, the state receives benefit from their training, as well as their contributions to its tax base.

SOME FUNDING MECHANISMS

Thus far, states have generally opted to support basic research through two funding mechanisms: research project grant programs and centers programs. In research project programs, funds are awarded to individual investigators to perform a specified piece of basic research via a competitive review and selection process. Centers programs make competitive awards to research centers and institutes.[2]

State-Sponsored Basic Research Grant Programs

A June 1989 report issued jointly by the National Governors' Association (NGA) and the National Science Foundation (NSF) indicated that 19 of the 45 competitive project grant programs included in the study supported basic research. In some cases, individual programs support a range of research from basic to development of commercial ideas and prototype development. In others, such as the Texas Advanced Research Program (ARP), the sole focus is basic research. Begun in 1987, ARP is intended to develop the basic research capabilities of the state's higher education institutions, and by the end of calendar year 1988 had received $20 million in state appropriations and initiated 144 projects selected in a competitive review process (Forrer 1989).

State-Sponsored Research Centers

According to the 1988 report of the Minnesota Department of Trade and Economic Development, 29 states operate research and technology centers. Although the majority of state center programs focus on applied research, technological innovation and development, and technology transfer, a few support basic research directly, while others sponsor research that bridges the gap between basic research performed at universities and potential industrial applications in marketable products (Office of Science and Technology 1988).

One state, Oklahoma, supports all three types of centers. Through its Centers of Excellence Program, Oklahoma funds Centers of Excellence for Basic Research and Centers of Excellence Incorporating Basic and Applied Research. The former support original investigation undertaken for the advancement of scientific knowledge. Although the research is not intended to have a specific commercial objective, it may have the potential of long-range commercial interest. In contrast, the Basic and Applied Research Centers are intended to engage in activities that include and blend basic and technological research to allow movement of ideas and results through the "gray" zone between basic and applied research. The overall program, which includes Centers of Excellence in Applied Research, Development, and Technology Transfer, was scheduled to make $11,754,450 worth of awards in FY 1989, and supports research in biotechnology; engineering; and natural, material, and computer sciences

(Oklahoma Center for the Advancement of Science and Technology 1988a, 1988b).

EXAMINING PROGRAM IMPACT

Confusion is evident with regard to why states have opted to support basic research. While state leaders who created such programs may understand the goals of their programs, it is not clear that others do. In 1986, the Research Policy Committee of the Committee for Economic Development (an independent research and educational organization created to propose policies to bring about steady economic growth) wrote: "Shifting too much responsibility to the state level from either the federal or the local level could obscure the legitimate and important responsibilities these other levels of government have in promoting healthy economies" (p. 80). Based on the variety of specific reasons that states have for creating science and technology programs and the degree to which the programs have been shaped to match state needs with existing assets, it is unclear that states have been motivated by a perception of shifting responsibility for economic development. This seems particularly so with respect to state support of basic research, since the federal government has not changed its stance on the importance of national support of basic research. Rather, states have come increasingly to understand that, just as the country benefits from federal support for basic research, states can also benefit from programs designed to meet their own economic needs and aspirations.

Determination of Success

Besides confusion regarding program goals, there is also confusion surrounding when and how to determine whether state programs are successful. Referring again to the 1986 Research Policy Committee report, the statement was made that "although state government in general has made impressive strides, differences in size, geography, demography, economic history, and political culture remain. Some states will do better in a more state-competitive environment; others will do less well, or perhaps their fortunes will decline" (p. 80). Differences in program components, size, scope, goals, eligibility requirements, and management mechanisms clearly reflect differences in state needs, resources, and philosophy. No doubt, some states will experience more positive effects as a result of their science and technology development programs than others. The hazard is that success will be judged by comparing one state's growth with that of another state. This is to be avoided at all costs, precisely because of the differences among states, state-wide programs, state needs, and state assets. Just as the relative priority given to the various goals for supporting basic research differs between the federal government and state governments, the mix from state to state also varies.

Success, especially with respect to the basic research components, must be viewed in terms of the goals and objectives of individual programs. It must also reflect the nature of basic research and the time element involved in this type of inquiry. Given the long-term return on investment that is intrinsic to basic research, it is particularly important that existing programs be allowed to continue for a sufficient amount of time before assessment of impact. For states, this will be a challenge, since technological innovation and development components tend to produce tangible short-term results. Nonetheless, it is fundamental if state programs that support basic research are to have a chance to contribute to economic development.

Ultimately, the success of individual state efforts to support basic research must be evaluated in terms of the degree to which they accomplish the economic development goals that they were intended to address. As distasteful as the term "accountability" is to researchers and state program administrators who fear that their programs will be inappropriately reviewed by evaluators, the principle of obtaining desirable outcomes from the expenditure of public funds is sound. This is particularly true when those funds are precious, the opportunity costs of using them for basic research support are considerable, and tangible results are generally obtained more rapidly from research programs emphasizing application and technological development. In states where basic research programs are targeted at enhancing existing economic bases or developing new strengths, identifying economic impact is more likely to be a clear-cut task. There is no doubt that there are intangible benefits to conducting basic research; nonetheless, the economic stakes are too high in most states to allow spending on basic research to take place in the absence of identifiable economic benefit accruing from the investment.

Attribution of Impact

Procedurally, evaluation of basic research programs has two dimensions: (1) to balance the need for timely information with recognition that they must be allowed to develop over a longer period of time than is required for other types of R&D programs; and (2) to base the evaluation on appropriate measures of impact. From a methodological standpoint, one pitfall into which a premature impact assessment can plunge is mistaking the technical development of the mechanics of a program, especially if it contains centers, with actual productivity of the program's supported activities. Demonstrating that centers have hired a certain number of personnel and purchased specific pieces of equipment are indicators of development of program infrastructure, not productivity. Another pitfall involves identifying such measures as the number of jobs produced as a result of a given program as indicators of the economic benefit of the program. Counting the number of jobs in different sectors in a state is not especially difficult; attributing cause and effect is an entirely different matter.

The ways in which state leaders have chosen to support basic research indicate a desire to carve out a role for basic research that is consistent with state goals. Thus, state emphasis on economic development and competitiveness has brought about a focus on collaboration among different types of research. Support for "gray zone" research is understandable and demonstrates recognition of specific research opportunities with strategic importance to states. At the same time, the existence of these programs reflects a gradual dissolution of discrete boundaries between types of scientific and technological inquiry. Collaborative R&D efforts between public and private entities have increased awareness among many that such distinctions are no longer descriptive of the universe of research.

The result is a strain on traditional R&D taxonomies or models of program operation. Evaluating the impact of programs that bridge standard boundaries requires making difficult methodological decisions about attribution of impact because, without standard taxonomic distinctions, established rules of thumb for selecting appropriate measures do not apply. Further, choosing an appropriate period of delay after the program has commenced before conducting an evaluation is a more complex process than averaging the "normal" time for discrete basic and applied programs. In both instances, it may not be possible to break out distinct effects of the different types of research because the distinctions are artificial in the particular program settings.

The goals of public support for basic research described at the outset suggest a number of possible impact indicators. One series of measures pertains to where those who worked on individual grants and in centers or institutes as undergraduates, graduate students, and postdoctoral fellows obtained their first jobs at the completion of their training, what types of positions they took, and what their highest degree was. Tracking participants provides an indication of the degree to which the state ultimately benefits from the training it provided. Economic benefit can be demonstrated when companies and higher education institutions become less dependent upon importing scientific and technological talent to maintain or enhance quality and competitiveness. It is also evident when more people who obtained scientific and technological training in a given state choose to work in the state when they complete their education.

Another series of economic development measures relate to collaborations between basic researchers and industry in the state. For centers and institutes, this is a particularly appropriate indicator. When collaborations are successful, there is a synergism among participants such that the nature of both the research and the results are of a scope not consistent with what a series of individual efforts would produce. Looking at collaborations involves charting not only expenditures and counting agreements; it also involves qualitative review of the nature of the work involved and identifying results of the research, be they a new process or new understanding of a phenomenon, upon which the industrial sector is able to capitalize commercially.

Resisting Temptation

A 1987 workshop on strategies for states to assess their science and technology programs—cosponsored by the Government-University-Industry Research Roundtable, NGA, and the National Research Council—concluded that many problems stem from two state-level audiences with different agendas. Specifically, officials who allocate resources are most interested in short-term quantitative data related to the programs' ultimate, long-term goal of economic development, "such as the numbers of new jobs the program has created in the state, the number of start-up firms helped by the program, and the number of new patents it has generated" (Government-University-Industry Research Roundtable 1987, 6 [hereafter G-U-I 1987]). Conversely, officials who manage the programs are interested in data—often qualitative—on progress toward achieving proximate goals, such as strengthening graduate education and university research.

Those who deal with resources put pressure on program managers to provide inappropriate data, which is of no net benefit and proves no one's case. Program officials are reluctant to provide quantitative economic impact data not only because the measures are incorrect, but also because "a cause and effect relationship between these programs and economic development cannot be ascertained directly because there is no experimental control to show what would have happened in the state if the program did not exist" (G-U-I 1987, 5).

The workshop concluded that program officials should set reasonable goals to limit the potential for failure, and that they should put their efforts into convincing state legislatures that their programs will benefit economic development in the long term (G-U-I 1987). While this advice is based in the practical fact that if program officers do not give the legislatures the data that they want they place their programs in jeopardy, they are probably doing so anyway when they supply inappropriate data. This is particularly true in the case of programs that support basic research. Of all types of research, it requires the most time to bring about impact.

An alternative approach is for program officials to resist going the easier route of providing inappropriate data and launch a vigorous education effort in their state legislatures. This would entail clear delineation of: the nature of basic research, proximate and ultimate goals, appropriate measures of progress for each in the context of basic research, and the legitimacy of qualitative data for decision making.

Evaluation of basic research programs presents formidable political and methodological challenges. This does not, however, lead to the conclusion that it cannot be done properly in a way that satisfies both perspectives. It does mean that those who conduct the evaluation and those who act on the results of the evaluation need as much knowledge about the nature of basic research and how its impact can be studied as possible in order to ensure sound decision making. The programs deserve no less.

NOTES

1. Any opinions, findings, and conclusions or recommendations expressed in this publication are those of the author and do not necessarily reflect the views of the National Science Foundation.

2. In this chapter, the terms "center" and "institute" are considered synonymous and refer to discrete organizational units within a college or university, other than an academic department, that engage in task-oriented multidisciplinary or interdisciplinary basic research per Ikenberry and Friedman (1972).

REFERENCES

Bloch, Erich. 1986. *Basic research: The key to economic competitiveness.* Washington, DC: National Science Foundation. NSF-86–21.

Forrer, John. 1989. *State competitive research grant programs.* Washington, DC: National Governors' Association and National Science Foundation.

Government-University-Industry Research Roundtable, National Governors' Association, and National Research Council. 1987. *State government strategies for self-assessment of science and technology programs for economic development.* Washington, DC: National Academy Press.

Ikenberry, Stanley O. and R. C. Friedman. 1972. *Beyond academic departments: The story of institutes and centers.* San Francisco: Jossey-Bass.

Minnesota Department of Trade and Economic Development. 1988. *State technology programs in the United States: 1988.* Report by the Office of Science and Technology, July.

National Science Foundation. 1991. *Benefits of basic research.* Washington, DC: National Science Foundation.

Oklahoma Center for the Advancement of Science and Technology. 1988a. *OCAST program update: A status report on programs.* Oklahoma City: Oklahoma Center for the Advancement of Science and Technology.

———. 1988b. *Oklahoma Centers of Excellence Program 1989 program solicitation.* Oklahoma City: Oklahoma Center for the Advancement of Science and Technology.

Research and Policy Committee. 1986. *Leadership for dynamic state economies.* New York: Committee for Economic Development.

III Changing Policy Issues

8 Recent Theoretical and Organizational Approaches to U.S. Technology Policy

Irwin Feller

The federal government, surrounded by continuing challenges to the U.S. competitive position in R&D-intensive fields, has established new programs to accelerate the commercialization of federally funded research and research performed by mission agencies and to foster university-industry R&D collaboration. The theoretical parameters that have bounded much of U.S. technology policy have been subjected to increasing criticism. Hemmed between continuing skepticism about the ability of government programs to target commercial R&D programs and systemic pressures for demonstrated effectiveness and efficiency, new technology programs are subjected to evaluations early in their history.

Each of these statements is found in a loosely connected form amid oft-expressed and widely shared diagnoses of the U.S. parlous technological competitiveness in the new global economy. However, for the most part these statements are formally analyzed or filtered into policy as three discrete modes of discourse. Theoretical arguments on the appropriateness of government support of civilian technology are seldom extended into discussions of organizational design or program implementation. In a related manner, analyses of inter- and intraorganizational aspects of program implementation focus on improving program performance, but not necessarily on a program's consistency with efficiency or equity criteria for governmental action. Evaluations are organized about program objectives that embody implicit behavioral models and legislative compromises, with little historical comprehension of the dynamics of adding new missions to existing organizations or of inserting new organizations into the programmatic or resource space claimed by existing organizations.

This chapter integrates these modes of discourse. It explores the inter-dependent nature of theories of technological innovation, organizational design, and institutional innovation as elements in the formulation of U.S. technology policy.

CONTEMPORARY TECHNOLOGY POLICY DISCOURSE

Determination of the appropriateness of (increased) government actions targeted at the commercialization of new products and processes, and increases in manufacturing productivity, typically pass through two ana-lytical filters on their way to program selection. First, some form of government action is necessary to offset market failure or departures from competitively determined outcomes. Second, mechanisms and organiza-tions that will lead to sought-after improvements without falling victim to well-understood maladies of government failure (Wolf 1988) can be designed and operated.

The first filter connects with current debates in economics about con-tending theoretical approaches to the conditions under which government support of various forms of research and development can improve social welfare. The policy significance of this debate stems from the dominant role played by the neoclassical paradigm of appropriability/property rights in shaping federal policies toward the support of civilian technologies.

The framework has provided a stylized but serviceable outline for federal science and technology policy during much of the post–World War II period. In the first pressing from the academic to the policy worlds, theoretical propositions on the economics of basic research stated that divergences between social and private rates of return and the inability of private actors to appropriate returns from their investments in such re-search would cause a societal underinvestment in basic research (Nelson, Peck, and Kalachek 1967). The analysis simultaneously held that private firms could be expected to appropriate sufficient returns for applied research to make public-sector investment unnecessary.[1]

The second filter draws from the prevailing diagnosis that America's failure to maintain its technological leadership and the associated macro-economic woes of declining international competitiveness, deteriorating trade balances, and slow rates of economic growth follow from the nation's failure to convert its vaunted lead in scientific research into commercially competitive products.[2] The common prescription following this diagnosis is to add more of a diffusion-orientation to a national policy characterized by a mission orientation. As Ergas (1987, 232) notes, "the key problem of technology policy (as distinguished from science policy) lies less in generating new ideas than in ensuring that they are effectively used." These prescriptions share two common ingredients. The first is the establishment of closer working relationships between and among public- and private-sector organizations involved in the generation of new knowledge and the transformation of this knowledge into commercial products and processes. The second is the acceleration of the rate at which new technologies are incorporated into the private sector's product lines and production processes. Reorientation of domestic technology policy to the effective commercial utilization of new ideas, by general consent, also involves altering the missions of existing organizations and/or creating new organizations to undertake these activities.

THEORETICAL BASIS OF U.S. TECHNOLOGY POLICY DEBATES

Debates on the need for and contents of a U.S. technology policy have had a Manichaean cast between theoretical rectitude—which stiffens public-sector resolve not to yield to the rent-seeking behavior of firms, workers, and technology advocates—and pragmatic responses to the technology and trade policies of other countries.

Dominating the theoretical high ground in these debates have been propositions drawn heavily from the work of economists that legitimize government support of technological innovation to provide new or improved technology for public-sector functions (e.g., defense) or in specific, limited situations of "market failure." Most frequently, these situations have been defined in terms of (and restricted to) the riskiness of certain types of research, the difficulties of establishing property rights in selected forms of new knowledge, the presence of externalities, and (increasingly) to the ratio of capital costs of a project to the resources available to a firm (or industry) (Nelson 1959; Arrow 1962; Dasgupta 1987). In the absence of these conditions, public-sector resource allocation generates economic rents to firms or users who would otherwise have sufficient incentives to contract for the R&D necessary to offset the technical and economic uncertainties surrounding the transformation of knowledge into new products and processes.

Reinforcing this line of analysis are generic propositions that the public-sector supply of goods and services is prone to overproduction (relative to a socially optimal quantity) and to the use of inefficient methods of production. These propositions imply that government agencies, congressional committees, and some mix of academic scientists or industrial representatives constitutes a "high tech" version of an iron triangle to promote new technologies. As applied to technology policy decisions, public-sector decisionmakers are held to confront different payoffs from risk-taking and profit-maximizing behavior than do private-sector decisionmakers. Accordingly, they are vulnerable to the selection of the wrong technologies or, confronted with trade-offs between development resources and development time, to the selection of an unduly rapid pace of development (Scherer 1965).

Support for these propositions is readily found in the numerous historical examples of the flawed and ineffective character of governmental efforts to promote the commercial development of specific technologies (Quigley 1982; White 1982). In their account of the federal government's flirtation with advanced nuclear power reactors and supersonic transportation, Eads and Nelson (1971) observed that pressures to develop these technologies came from government agencies and congressional committees, not from the relevant industries. Cohen and Noll (1991, 255) describe the Clinch River Breeder Reactor program as "the quintessential example of a technological turkey by the time it was mercifully put to rest in 1983." They note, too, the influence of distributive politics that kept Congress funding the program after the leftward shift in demand for electricity caused the bottom to fall out of the economic justifications for the program.

Roessner's account of U.S. government efforts to develop and commercialize solar technology likewise noted several mismatches between the status of selected solar energy technologies and the strategies used by government to stimulate their development. Echoing themes voiced by Don Price in his characterization of the baneful effects of the political estate on what were then delimited as science policy issues, Roessner (1984, 245) cites political benefits that public officials believed would be garnered from "highly visible, easily implementable, short-term programs that touched as many different constituencies as possible" as one cause of the mismatch. More recently, failure of government policymakers to heed what Mowery (1983, 28) has termed "the important role of intrafirm research expertise in enabling a firm to exploit extramural research" has led British science and technology policymakers to adopt plausible, even fashionable, modes of support, such as research consortia for precompetitive research that have not achieved stated policy objectives. Reports, for example, on Britain's Alvey program, undertaken with high hopes as an example of a broad-based interrelated approach to precompetitive research and development in the field of information technology (Freeman 1987), now suggest that the program's research goals have been met, but that this research has been infrequently used by Britain's information technology industry (Bird 1991).

Submerged in these otherwise compelling cases against government targeting of civilian technology development have been analytical reformulations of the case(s) for public sector-action to affect the rate and direction of technical progress. At least three lines of analysis that bear upon contemporary technology policy debates have emerged as modifications and extensions of the neoclassical R&D paradigm. The first two lines of analysis—increasing returns to scale and strategic trade policy—most directly relate to government decisions to support the development of new commercially oriented technologies. The third—technology transfer—more closely relates to the diagnosis of the need to build new inter-organizational channels to foster the commercialization of new technological knowledge.

Increasing Returns to Scale

The increasing returns argument presents the case for technology policy as a means of preventing a rival's initial leads from being converted into an unclosable distance. In contrast to the long-standing propositions that followers enjoy opportunities to imitate leaders and therefore need not be concerned about falling from the position of leader to (fast) follower, this line of analysis concludes that the race may be won by the swiftest, but that the swiftest need not be the (technical) best. The presence of increasing returns to adoption implies that "a technology that by chance gains an early lead in adoption may eventually 'corner the market' of potential adopters, with the other technologies becoming locked out" (Arthur 1989, 116). According to Arthur (p. 122), increasing returns might drive the adoption process into developing a technology that has inferior long-run potential: "An early run of agenttypes who prefer an initially attractive but slow-to-improve technology can lock the market into this inferior option; equal development of the excluded technology in the long run would pay off better to both types." In such a situation, public-sector subsidization of a second-system option may be needed to encourage continuation of private R&D devoted to creating new variants or fundamentally enhancing the older ones. The dynamics of this process are illustrated by Paul David's (1985) compelling account of the appearance and hegemony of QWERTY, the omnipresent keyboard layout, in the face of competition from "technically" superior alternatives.

The policy implications arising from this type of technological dynamic are ambiguous, however. The prospect of a new technology characterized by strong network properties that can be locked in creates what David has termed the Blind Giant's Quandary, a situation in which "public agencies are likely to be at their most powerful in exercising influence upon the future trajectory of a network technology just when they know least about what should be done" (p. 230).

Strategic Trade Policy

A related set of arguments for public support of the development of commercial technologies has been derived from the recent literature on strategic trade policy. This literature extends the analysis of oligopolistic firms competing in world markets to consider the impacts of governmental export promotion and import restriction policies on the "games" and the "strategic" choices made by firms and nations. Under this framework, a more extensive and somewhat different set of impacts is predicted for government policies than in mainstream trade theory. In mainstream trade theory, for example, government subsidization of a firm's costs may make it more profitable for a (domestic firm) to expand output, thereby displacing foreign imports or sales to Third World countries. To the extent that the original share of world markets held by domestic and foreign firms represents competitively determined costs, the shift from foreign to domestic production serves to increase the profits of the domestic firms and to lower those of the foreign firms. The subsidy, however, represents in part a transfer of income from the (domestic) society at large to the protected industry.

The outcome may be different in a strategic trade policy world comprised of oligopolistic firms. Faced with a credible or believable threat that domestic firms will expand output (as a consequence of a government subsidy), a rival firm's best (profit-maximizing) response is to contract output; this contraction raises the domestic firm's profit by an additional amount (Brander 1988, 29). Total profits may exceed the amount of the subsidy, thereby increasing total (domestic) income. Moreover, if economies of scale occur in the production of technology, trade policies that expand exports and limit imports combine to both increase the productivity of domestic firms' R&D and decrease (through contracting market size) the productivity of foreign firms (Lyons 1987).

Brander has highlighted the implications of this line of reasoning for domestic technology policy through the example of the next generation of wide-body jet aircraft. He argues that two but not three firms will be able to make substantial profits from the next generation of these aircraft: "Boeing will probably be one of the 'winners'; the other contenders are

McDonnell-Douglas, Lockheed and the European entrant (Airbus). Subsidization of the European entrant gives that firm an edge." Such a subsidy may serve to persuade McDonnell-Douglas and Lockheed not to try to enter the market, thus making it possible for it to "more than pay for itself in the form of profits or other rents" (Brander 1988, 31).

Thus, both the increasing returns and the strategic trade policy approaches point to a similar conclusion: rather than constituting rent to firms, government support for the development of a civilian technology may be necessary to stimulate the optimal quantity of private-sector R&D.

Technology Transfer

The third approach emphasizes the institutional structure of a nation's R&D system as a determinant of its ability to realize the economic benefits from public- and private-sector research. It further contends that the appropriability framework that has legitimized government support of basic research but barred support of civilian technologies is an inadequate guide for whether sufficient market incentives exist to encourage private actors to invest in the generation of new knowledge and its conversion into commercializable products. The shortcoming of the appropriability framework is held to be its sole emphasis on the generation of new knowledge and its failure to address the transmission and utilization of research findings. According to Mowery and Rosenberg (1989, 293), "the utilization and diffusion of scientific and engineering research should receive greater weight within R&D policy."

This framework emphasizes institutional arrangements and the importance of internal and external knowledge-generating and -processing activities within and among organizations. An organization must possess the capacity to process its own internally generated new knowledge. Because new technology, as Mowery (1983, 31) has written, does not constitute a page from a book of blueprints; but rather, "a complex mix of codified data and poorly-defined 'know-how,' " a firm must be able to assimilate and utilize knowledge generated by other organizations.

In many respects, this formulation captures the essence of much of the contemporary diagnosis of and prescriptions for U.S. technology policy. Its distinctive contribution is its emphasis on the requirements for complementary actions by firms if the externally offered technological knowledge supplied by new publicly supported programs is to be used effectively. Pregnant with policy implications, the above three lines of analysis have been developed and debated primarily at the theoretical level. They have not included much historical, empirical, or political elaboration. Grossman, for example, has faulted the strategic trade policy approach precisely for this reason. He has argued that targeted export promotion policies (such as subsidization of R&D) derived from the strategic trade model run the risk of falling prey to the same sort of special-interest pressures that have characterized trade policy more generally. "Market failures in the political realm," he argues, "might easily outweigh those in the economic realm, leaving us with a set of strategic trade policies that would serve only the interests of those fortunate enough to gain favor" (Grossman 1988, 65). Similarly, current treatments by economists of the importance of new institutional arrangements cite new programs and approaches to bridge the generation, transfer, and assimilation of knowledge as encouraging steps along new, right-policy paths,[3] but do not delve deeply into issues relating to organizational design and the political and performance standards of government and private R&D laboratories (Bozeman and Crow 1991). Schankerman (1990, 1761) has aptly characterized the policy prescriptions drawn by economists from their recent theoretical treatments of the subsidization of R&D as ignoring "the need to construct organizational structures that allow for the effective transmission of complex research results and technological information."

INSTITUTIONS, ORGANIZATIONS, AND PROGRAMS

What is involved in creating a new set of institutional arrangements that are effective in the sense of accelerating the rate of technological change, efficient in the sense of yielding social rates of return that satisfy public investment criteria, and stable in the sense that they can generate the necessary degree of political support to receive continued funding? What type of programs and which organizations are best equipped to operationalize the above precepts of theoretical rectitude and institutional design? Should government laboratories be required to take on additional technology transfer roles, as under Stevenson-Wydler; should new entities be created, such as NIST's Manufacturing Technology Centers or Michigan's Industrial Technology Institute? Should renewed attention be given to government-supported industrial research institutes, an important element among competing nations but a stepchild of U.S. technology policy (Crow, Emmert, and Jacobson 1990)? The analytical frameworks used by economists are of little value to policymakers in answering these questions.

Recognizing this, economists who study technological innovation have increasingly begun to speak of the institutional infrastructure that supports a nation's scientific and technological innovation capabilities. The problem of designing institutions to promote technological innovation has been clearly stated by Nelson (1988, 315): Establish and preserve property rights, at least to some degree, where profit incentives are effective in stimulating action, and where the costs of keeping knowledge private are not high. Share knowledge where it is of high cost not to do so, and the cost in terms of diminished incentives is small. Do the work cooperatively, or fund it publicly, and make public those aspects of technology where the advantages of open access are greatest, or where proprietary claims are the most difficult to police. Put another way, the design problem involves institutional creation and task assignment at least as much as simple trade-offs taking institutional structure as given. Economists also have articulated a definition of institutions that is sufficiently encompassing to include the iterative, interconnected links in technological innovation. Ruttan and Hayami (1984, 204), for example, define institutions as

the rules of a society or of organizations that facilitate coordination among people by helping them form expectations which each person can reasonably hold in dealing with others. They reflect the conventions that have evolved in different societies regarding the behavior of individuals and groups relative to their own behavior and the behavior of others.

In its incorporation of both formal and informal rules, emphasis on interdependency and on evolution, this definition in many ways captures the zeitgeist of the Rosenberg-Mowery-Nelson strain of analysis.

Missing from economists' work on the characteristics of institutions, however, is an examination of the functioning of organizations. Moreover, their concept of institutions is too broad, long-term, and elusive to be useful within the political, pragmatic, and incremental scope within which public sector decisions are made.

Researchers in other disciplines and participants in national science and technology debates have a longer tradition of using programs and organizations as the conceptual building blocks of their analysis of U.S. technology policy. As Lambright (1976, 4) has noted, "the technoscience agencies are at the heart of the Federal R&D function. . . . [They] are where the action is—whether they wish to be or not." Thus, most studies of government science and technology policy have tended to be couched in analytical frameworks derived from organizational theory, or as case histories or evaluations of the effectiveness of specific programs.

These studies also frequently challenge the conceptual organizing blocks within which most economists have worked. Barry Bozeman and Michael Crow (1990; Crow and Bozeman 1987), for example, have contended that existing typologies of public- and private-sector R&D

laboratories fail to adequately describe the relative degrees to which laboratories respond to market, political, or scientific signals, and do not adequately account for the determinants of a laboratory's effective performance of its research and technology transfer activities.

Implicit in every debate over the appropriateness of a specific domestic technology program is an analysis of the need to add new missions to existing organizations, the need for new organizations, and the mix between these two strategies. Inserting programs into existing organizations, however, raises questions about the importance attached to the new mission and related activities. As Lambright and Teich (1976, 31) have argued, "establishing a [technology] delivery system requires overcoming the fragmentation of institutional actors performing the various functions required in transfer. The actors must be linked with one another in different ways at various times during the transfer process." Attempts to move laboratories into different "environmental niches," "may prove fatal to the laboratories being reoriented and may damage the overall laboratory system" (Bozeman and Crow 1990, 49).

The susceptibility of organizations to the ailments of reorientation is already visible in interim accounts of recent initiatives. Crow, Emmert, and Jacobson (1990, 73) note that congressional attempts to increase the market relevance of government research laboratories, whose primary mission has been basic science, may potentially be dysfunctional. "Public science labs, unlike public technology labs, produce much of the basic knowledge and infratechnology by which technology-oriented research is driven. Instead of redirecting public science laboratories, policymakers need to consider expanding the application of public technology labs" (p. 73). The U.S. Office of Technology Assessment report, *Making Things Better* (1990, 191), also notes that the collaborative incentives between federal laboratories and industry "are sometimes weak or even negative." Laboratories are unlikely "to embrace technology transfer enthusiastically if they have no money to pay for it. . . . Time spent answering a firm's questions is usually time spent away from research; and help to industry does not always count in a researcher's performance evaluation, even though the law specifically directs that it should."

The appearance of these observations—and the increased frequency with which they are likely to be made as fuller documentation of recent programs appears—is the stuff of forthcoming political battles, given the ideological environment surrounding technology policy debates. What is striking, however, about the above recitations of the intra- and inter-organizational problems encountered in recent technology policy initiatives is their resonance with the evolution of the U.S. public agricultural technology delivery system. This system is repeatedly extolled as a model of a successful public-sector R&D system. It provides an integrated technology system that links a critical mass of new technology, a research subsystem oriented to utilization, a high-degree of user control over the research utilization system, and structural linkages among the research utilization system's components (NSF 1983, 163).

However, at no time in the past, nor indeed at present, has this integration occurred without stress (Feller 1986). Obscured by familiarity and documented success is the length of time required to establish the organizations that comprise the agricultural technology delivery system: 52 years elapsed between the passage of the Morrill Act in 1862 and the SmithLever Act in 1914. Historically, each piece of legislation (Morrill Act, 1982, Hatch Act, 1887, Adams Act, 1906, and SmithLever Act, 1914) was then subject to considerable debate about the roles of each organization in this system. More salient to current policy debates, each of these acts was designed in part to compensate for the failure of each prior bill to generate the association between research and technology transfer sought by both performers and users of research (Marcus 1985, 1986; Rosenberg 1964, 1971; Scott 1970).

CONCLUSION

U.S. technology policy remains beset by fixity and flexibility, and by uncertainty in regard to both program design and program implementation.

The fixed point remains an unwillingness to support the "targeting" of specific commercially oriented technologies, except mainly when some association can be made between the technology or its underlying manufacturing processes and national defense. The rationale continues, for example, to call into question the justification for the U.S. Department of Commerce's Advanced Technology Program, which provides funding to U.S. businesses and consortia for the development of precompetitive, generic technologies on the grounds that market failure has not been demonstrated. It also provides a formidable obstacle to calls for federal support of high-definition television (*New York Times* 1989, A18) on the grounds that the private sector is better able to determine the level and rate at which funds should be committed to R&D as well as to select the research questions to be answered.

The flexibility is found in the federal government's willingness to support the establishment of new relationships between and among federal, state, industrial, and university suppliers and users of new knowledge, all with a view toward accelerating the commercial introduction of new technologies. Contemporary U.S. technology policy constitutes a search for the right mix of industries, technologies, organizational performers, and incentives. New technology programs are an array of ad hoc arrangements, most with uncertain impact and prospects for continuation. More pointedly at this date, the relationships between program impacts and program continuation are unclear. A sense of victory over a recalcitrant executive branch and the protective spirit that envelops fledgling undertakings nurtures recent U.S. technology initiatives. At some point, however, attention will begin to focus on the extent to which these policy innovations comprise a set of interconnected activities and programs capable of generating a nationally acceptable rate of technological innovation. Interconnections do not need to be "planned" or formally coordinated as such to exist. They may evolve from the interaction of discrete programs, organizations, and sections to produce a workable and effective "technology delivery system" (Ezra 1975) for a technology cluster, an industry, or a nation.

Establishing a linked set of activities among research and technology transfer units within, between, and among organizations is a formidable and long-term task, as suggested by the history of the U.S. agricultural R&D system. The task requires critical attention to the initial selection of organizations and missions, and a willingness to displace organizational arrangements that do not work with other ones, including, as needed, the establishment of new organizations. It also requires redress from pressures for short-term results. Finally, it likely requires longer-term commitments of federal funding for "experimental" programs than are available at present.

NOTES

1. The stylized character of this framework has long been evident, specifically the positing of operationally precise demarcations between basic and applied research that do not exist. The private sector finances and conducts basic research while the public sector finances and performs applied research (Mansfield 1980). Private-sector support for basic research has been found to yield high private rates of return, suggesting that whatever leakages occur in the ability of firms to appropriate economic benefits or of excesses of social over private rates of return, sufficiently high rates of return still remain to warrant investment. Economists, although generally eschewing targeting of R&D for specific technologies or industries, have nevertheless formulated criteria, such as institutional barriers that limit R&D by private firms (e.g., small firms), and the high social value of rapid technology progress in a particular technology or industry, under which this support can be efficient.

2. As Dertouzos et al. (1989, 67) note, "the United States is still unarguably the leader in basic research. The scale of its scientific enterprise is unequaled, and it is second to none in making new discoveries. Yet U.S. companies increasingly find themselves lagging behind their foreign rivals in the commercial exploitation of inventions and discoveries."

3. "[t]he key policy problem will be to augment or redesign institutions rather than to achieve particular resource allocations per se. . . . [T]he policy search must be for a set of institutions that will allocate resources appropriately over a wide range of circumstances and time" (Nelson and Winter 1977, 40).

REFERENCES

Arrow, Kenneth. 1962. Economic welfare and the allocation of resources for invention. In R. Nelson, ed., *The Rate and Direction of Inventive Activity*. Princeton, NJ: Princeton University Press.

Arthur, W. Brian. 1989. Competing technologies, increasing returns, and lock-in by historical events. *Economic Journal* 99: 116–131.

Bird, Jane. 1991. Britain picks wrong way to beat the Japanese. *Science* 252 (31 May): 1248.

Bozeman, Barry and Michael Crow. 1990. The environments of U.S. R&D laboratories: political and market influences. *Policy Sciences* 23: 25–56.

———— . Technology transfer from U.S. government and university R&D laboratories. *Technovation* 11 (4):231–246..

Brander, James. 1988. Rationales for strategic trade and industrial policy. In Paul Krugman, ed., *Strategic trade policy and the new international economics*. Cambridge, MA: MIT Press, pp. 23– 46.

Cohen, Linda and Roger Noll. 1991. *The technology pork barrel*. Washington, DC: Brookings Institution.

Crow, Michael and Barry Bozeman. 1987. A new typology for R&D laboratories: implications for policy analysis. *Journal of Policy Analysis and Management* 6: 328–341.

Crow, Michael, Mark Emmert, and Carol Jacobson. 1990. Government-supported industrial research institutes in the United States. *Policy Studies Journal* (Fall): 59–74.

Dasgupta, Partha. 1987. The economic theory of technology policy: An introduction. In Partha Dasgupta and Paul Stoneman, eds., *Economic theory and technological performance*. Cambridge: Cambridge University Press, p. 723.

David, Paul. 1987. New standards for the economics of standardization. In Partha Dasgupta and Paul Stoneman, eds., *Economic theory and technological performance*. Cambridge: Cambridge University Press, pp. 206–239.

Dertouzos, Michael, Richard Lester, Robert Solow, and the MIT Commission on Industrial Productivity. 1989. *Made in America.* Cambridge, MA: MIT Press.

Eads, George and Richard Nelson. 1971. Government support of advanced civilian technology: Power reactors and the supersonic transport. *Public Policy* 19: 405–428.

Ergas, Henry. 1987. Does technology policy matter? In Bruce Guile and Harvey Brooks, eds., *Technology and global industry.* Washington, DC: National Academy of Engineering, pp. 191–245.

Ezra, Arthur. 1975. Technology utilization: Incentives and solar energy. *Science* 28 (February): 707–713.

Feller, Irwin. 1986. Research and technology transfer linkages in agriculture. In Lawrence Busch and William Lacy, eds., *The agricultural scientific enterprise: A system in transition.*: Boulder, CO: Westview Press, pp. 280–295.

Freeman, Christopher. 1987. *Technology policy and economic performance.* London: Pinter Publishers.

Grossman, Gene. 1988. Strategic export promotion: A critique. In Paul Krugman, ed., *Strategic trade policy and the new international economics.* Cambridge, MA: MIT Press, pp. 47–68.

Lambright, W. Henry. 1976. *Governing science and technology.* New York: Oxford University Press.

Lambright, W. Henry and Albert Teich. 1976. Technology transfer as a problem in interorganizational relationships. *Administration and Society* 8: 29–54.

Lyons, Bruce. 1987. International trade and technology policy. In Partha Dasgupta and Paul Stoneman, eds., *Economic theory and technological performance.* Cambridge: Cambridge University Press, pp. 168–205.

Mansfield, E. 1980. Basic research and productivity increase in manufacturing. *American Economic Review* 70: 863–873.

Marcus, Alan. 1985. *Agricultural science and the quest for legitimacy.* Ames: Iowa State University Press.

————. 1986. From state chemistry to state science: The transformation of the idea of the agricultural experiment station, 1875–1887. In Lawrence Busch and William Lacy, eds., *The agricultural scientific enterprise: A system in transition.* Boulder, CO: Westview Press, pp. 3–12.

Mowery, David. 1983. Economic theory and government technology policy. *Policy Sciences* 16: 27–43.

———— and Nathan Rosenberg. 1989. *Technology and the pursuit of economic growth.* Cambridge: Cambridge University Press.

National Science Foundation. 1983. *The process of technological innovation: Reviewing the literature.* Washington, DC: National Science Foundation.

Nelson, Richard. 1959. The simple economics of basic scientific research. *Journal of Political Economy* 67 (3): 297–306.

————. 1988. Institutions supporting technical change in the U.S. In Giovanni Dosi, Christopher Freeman, Richard Nelson, Gerald Silverberg, and Luc Soete, eds., *Technical change and economic theory*. London: Pinter Publishers, pp. 312–329.

————, Merton Peck, and Edward Kalachek. 1967. *Economic growth and public policy*. Washington, DC: RAND Corporation and Brookings Institution.

Nelson, Richard and Sidney Winter. 1977. In search of a useful theory of innovation. *Research Policy* 6: 36–77.

New York Times 1989. Editorial: Should Uncle Sam tilt to HDTV? Yes: It's pivotal to industries of the future. May 15, p. 18A.

Quigley, John. 1982. Residential construction. In Richard Nelson, ed., *Government and technical progress*. New York: Pergamon Press, pp. 361–410.

Roessner, J. David. 1984. Commercializing solar technology: the government role. *Research Policy* 13: 235–246.

Rosenberg, Charles. 1964. The Adams Act: Politics and the cause of scientific research. *Agricultural History 38: 3–12.*

————. 1971. Science, technology, and economic growth: The case of the agricultural experiment station scientist, 1875–1914. *Agricultural History* 45: 1–20.

Ruttan, Vernon and Yujiro Hayami. 1984. Toward a theory of induced institutional innovation. *Journal of Development Studies* 20: 203–223.

Schankerman, Mark. 1990. Review of *Economic policy and technological performance*, edited by Partha Dasgupta and Paul Stoneman. *Journal of Economic Literature* 28: 1759–1761.

Scherer, Frederic. 1965. Government research and development programs. In Robert Dorfman, ed., *Measuring benefits of government investments*. Washington, DC: Brookings Institution, pp. 12–57.

Scott, Roy. 1970. *The reluctant farmer*. Urbana: University of Illinois Press.

U.S. Congress, Office of Technology Assessment. 1990. *Making things better: competing in manufacturing*. OTA-ITE-443. Washington, DC: U.S. Government Printing Office.

White, Lawrence. 1982. The motor vehicle industry. In Richard Nelson, ed., *Government and technical progress*. New York: Pergamon Press, pp. 411–440.

Wolf, Charles. 1988. *Markets or governments*. Cambridge, MA: MIT Press.

9 Changing International Relations and U.S.-Japanese Competitiveness

Maria Papadakis

U.S. technology-based competitiveness policies are typically grounded by a single dominating presumption about American international competitive decline: that U.S. technological leadership has eroded, and only intensive investments in basic science and industrial innovation can restore the U.S. position in the international marketplace. The belief is that a concentrated effort in the production of new technologies—and hence new industries and products—will restore technological advantage for the United States and reestablish a technology gap between itself and its major competitors. As has been well established in both theory and practice, the economic gains from monopolizing technology frontiers and the early stages of new product cycles are considerable.

Unfortunately, this manifest faith in the ability of technological leadership to rehone America's competitive edge is held in isolation of both subtle and dramatic changes in the international economy. Over the past 20 years the world production system has integrated to an unprecedented degree, with the result that technological advances are less and less likely to be the exclusive domain of any particular nation. The transnationalization of corporations, rising global technological and industrial capabilities, internationalization of the scientific community, and vast communication networks virtually assure the accelerated global diffusion of scientific discovery and technological advance. In short, as the international economy and marketplace become more integrated and interdependent, the creation and maintenance of technology gaps becomes increasingly difficult and notions of national technological ownership decreasingly relevant.

The purpose of this chapter is to explore the technological roots of U.S.-Japanese bilateral competitiveness and assess the implications of

Japan's contemporary technological advantage for policymaking. As will be seen, Japan's competitive performance may draw far more than suspected on fundamental changes in its manufacturing base, and it is complemented by a competitive strategy somewhat alien to the United States.

U.S. COMPETITIVENESS IN PERSPECTIVE, 1970–86

The closing of the technology gap (roughly in 1970) brought with it changes in the international competitive environment. *For the first time* in the international economic system, there were a significant number of foreign rivals in a large number of industries, and, because of growing similarities in national consumption patterns, vastly larger international markets to be exploited. International competitiveness was no longer to be crudely defined by a country's possession of exclusive manufacturing capacity and the associated domination of product cycles (in other words, by technology gaps); instead, the ability to prevail against foreign rivals in increasingly dynamic global markets became the new definition of competitive strength.

Around 1970 the United States was thus about to lose the immunity from import competition that it had enjoyed for the better part of 20 years. Two critical events of the early 1970s mark the final downfall of U.S. competitive isolation. For the first time a number of countries were able to enter into meaningful head-to-head competition over like products in multiple markets; additionally, the movement to flexible exchange rates eliminated the last significant barrier to widespread internationalization of markets. Far more than ever before, exchange rates would quickly reflect both the demand for foreign goods and the cost structures that produced them. By the early 1970s the world manufacturing economy was primed for a type of competition it had not experienced before, and economic mechanisms were being put in place that would allow a more rapid market expression of international competitive advantage.

One rather immediate result of the fully recovered postwar economies and the greater price sensitivity of traded goods was an explosion in world trade. The volume of international trade expanded considerably, so much so that U.S. merchandise exports as a percentage of domestic production more than doubled in eight years, from less than 10 percent to nearly 20 percent by 1980. Trading patterns in the decade following liberalization indicate that the industrialized countries *were* able to adjust to changed international competition. Even though the volume of trade, import penetration, and foreign competition in domestic markets grew considerably, overall balanced trade was maintained. This suggests that the industrialized countries were becoming increasingly differentiated and specialized in their comparative advantage as a means of sustaining gains from trade, a conclusion reinforced by the large volume of intraindustry trade between Europe, Japan, and the United States.

There is thus one critical point to appreciate about U.S. competitive performance after 1970: troubles didn't show up for virtually 12–13 years. Prior to the early 1980s the United States had experienced competitive distress, but it was principally confined to the steel, electronics, auto, and textile industries. Throughout the 1970s, criticisms of U.S. competitiveness typically took on an industry-specific flavor, and it wasn't until the onset of the competitiveness crisis—the dramatic worsening in the U.S. manufactures trade balance during 1982–83—that concerns about U.S. competitive ability instantaneously expanded to include the entire manufacturing sector. Assessing the validity of these concerns is nonetheless difficult, because the crisis can be reasonably attributed to at least three different sorts of economic problems: the U.S. macroeconomic recovery of 1982–83, a considerably overvalued U.S. dollar, and a serious erosion in the competitive abilities of U.S. business. As will be seen, much of the competitiveness crisis was nothing new, but simply a continuation of U.S. competitive decline among the four industries identified above. There are, however, some unique features of the crisis, specifically the magnitude of the competitive imbalance and the addition of several newly noncompetitive industries in the 1980s.

To evaluate the nature and causes of the competitiveness crisis, we need to be able to detect patterns in performance that will distinguish between systemic effects (e.g., leading business cycle recoveries, exchange rate values) and eroding competitive ability. By and large, trade patterns alone do this very well, but when combined with import penetration data, these data discriminate "core noncompetitiveness" from macroeconomic noise much more precisely. In general, poor trade performance from 1982–86 in all industries but aerospace provides some evidence of leading recovery effects (the same phenomenon could be observed in the mid-1970s); that the durable goods industries as a class were the worst performers is testimony to their price sensitivity and the overvalued dollar.

However, it does seem that "intrinsic" noncompetitiveness in a handful of industries accounts for virtually the full magnitude of the crisis. After 1982 there was an extraordinary trade decline in three industries that had been in competitive stress since the early 1970s: autos, textiles, and electronics. Declines by these sectors alone account for roughly one-half of the eroded balance of trade from 1982 to 1986, and together with steel

Table 9.1

Trends in the U.S. Balance of Trade, by Industrial Class, 1982–86 (dollars in millions)

Industry	Decline in balance, 1982-1986	Industry as a percent of total decline	Industry as a percent of 1986 deficit
Motor vehicles & equipment	($35,029)	24.5%	29.3%
Nonelectrical machinery	($20,976)	14.7%	1.7%
Textiles, footwear & leather	($16,553)	11.6%	16.0%
Electronic equipment & components	($13,848)	9.7%	10.8%
Electrical machinery	($7,832)	5.5%	3.6%
Fabricated metal products	($5,217)	3.6%	2.8%
Wood, cork & furniture	($4,824)	3.4%	4.2%
Office & computing machines	($4,654)	3.3%	NA
Other manufacturing	($4,648)	3.2%	4.8%
Chemicals	($4,457)	3.1%	NA
Food, drink, & tobacco	($4,320)	3.0%	4.0%
Rubber & plastic products	($3,989)	2.8%	3.6%
Instruments	($3,467)	2.4%	0.4%
Paper & printing	($3,201)	2.2%	2.3%
Stone, clay, & glass products	($3,099)	2.2%	2.2%
Non-ferrous metals	($3,079)	2.2%	3.4%
Other transportation equipment	($2,599)	1.8%	1.0%
Ferrous metals	($483)	0.3%	5.1%
Petroleum refining	($409)	0.3%	NA
Drugs & medicines	($386)	0.3%	NA
Not elsewhere classified	$608		
Aerospace	$1,395		NA
Total Deficit (or decline)	($143,070)		
Total surplus (or increase)	$2,003		

NA: These industries were still in surplus in 1986.

Source: Calculated by the author from OECD (1988).

they represent 61 percent of the total manufactures trade deficit in 1986 (see Table 9.1). In the past, deficits by these "Big 4" were offset by substantial surpluses in the electrical and nonelectrical machinery industries, surpluses that were lost entirely after 1982. The balance of trade reversal for the machinery industries, combined with the ongoing erosion of textiles, autos, and electronics, "explains" nearly 70 percent of the total decline in the U.S. trade balance from 1982 to 1986 and about 60 percent of the total 1986 deficit.

A juxtaposition of import penetration ratios (the percentage of domestic markets accounted for by foreign goods) with the trade trends reinforces

Table 9.2
Import Penetration of U.S. Manufactures Consumption, by Industrial Class, 1970–86

Industry	Import penetration ratio (%)		Percent of net change occurring in 1982-86	Type of Good
	1970	1986		
Other manufacturing	10.9	31.2	43.2	Durable
Motor vehicles & equipment	9.0	30.3	38.2	Durable
Office & computing machines	10.2	25.0	93.7	Durable
Textiles, footwear & leather	6.2	21.7	50.6	Non-durable
Electronic equipment & components	7.9	21.3	37.1	Durable
Instruments	6.8	18.6	45.6	Durable
Electrical machinery	3.5	17.3	48.0	Durable
Other transportation equipment	9.2	16.1	50.0	Durable
Nonferrous metals	10.3	14.8	29.2	Durable
Nonelectrical machinery	4.8	15.2	48.5	Durable
Wood, cork & furniture	6.5	13.5	55.4	Durable
Ferrous metals	7.0	13.2	-56.7	Durable
Aerospace	2.3	11.0	22.4	Durable
Rubber & plastic products	4.4	10.0	54.4	Non-durable
Stone, clay, & glass products	3.3	9.2	54.2	Durable
Chemicals	3.8	8.4	15.5	Non-durable
Drugs & medicines	1.4	6.6	45.1	Non-durable
Food, drink, & tobacco	4.8	5.4	65.8	Non-durable
Fabricated metal products	2.2	5.3	45.8	Durable
Petroleum refining	5.9	5.0	194.7	Non-durable
Paper & printing	3.5	4.3	66.6	Non-durable

Source: Calculated by the author from OECD (1988).

the picture of competitive decline in these industries. As illustrated in Tables 9.1 and 9.2, the most highly penetrated industries also tend to be those with the worst trade performance, indicating that imports were not flowing in to temporarily satisfy a recovering demand economy, but to displace domestic production: of the four major U.S. business cycles during 1970–86, the cycle beginning in 1982 accounts for a very disproportionate one-half of the net (1970–86) increase in import penetration of the durable goods industries. Exchange rate effects are also observable, since with the exception of textiles, the durable goods industries (which are relatively price elastic) are the worst competitive performers.

A competitive typology of the U.S. manufacturing sector suggests itself from the combined trade and import penetration trends. Generally, manufacturing industries can be classified as either core noncompetitive (suffering from trade deficits and high import penetration since the early

Table 9.3
Competitiveness Indicators for U.S. Manufacturing Industries, by Competitive Status

Industry	Import penetra-tion	Trade balance status	Technology class	Revealed comparative advantage [1]		
				'72	'82	'86
I. CORE NON-COMPETITIVE						
Motor vehicles & equipment	30.3%	largest deficit	medium	100	70	74
Textiles, footwear & leather	21.7%	2nd largest deficit	low	38	48	41
Electronic equipment & components	21.3%	3rd largest deficit	high	104	116	111
Ferrous metals	13.2%	4th largest deficit	low	32	24	16
Other manufacturing	31.2%	6th largest deficit	medium	88	69	63
Other transportation	16.1%	16th largest deficit	low	NA	75	80
Non-ferrous metals	14.8%	11th largest deficit	medium	60	71	61
Wood, cork & furniture	13.5%	7th largest deficit	low	70	74	77
II. NEWLY NON-COMPETITIVE						
Instruments	18.6%	reversal from surplus	high	143	144	144
Electrical machinery	17.3%	reversal from surplus	high	108	108	91
Nonelectrical machinery	15.2	reversal from surplus	medium	133	137	106
Office & computing machines	25.0	declining surplus	high	186	217	205
III. AT-RISK COMPETITIVE						
Rubber & plastic products	10.0%	worsening deficit	medium	67	61	69
Stone, clay, & glass products	9.2%	worsening deficit	low	61	61	55
Fabricated metal products	5.3%	reversal from surplus	low	80	78	56
IV. COMPETITIVE						
Aerospace	11.0%	stable surplus	high	343	242	340
Chemicals	8.4%	declining surplus	medium	112	111	107
Drugs & medicines	6.6%	declining surplus	high	105	109	142
Food, drink, & tobacco	5.4%	worsening deficit	low	104	95	105
Petroleum refining	5.0%	improving deficit	low	59	77	88
Paper & printing	4.3%	worsening deficit	low	102	101	105

[1] Based on OECD-11. A value of 100 represents no comparative advantage or disadvantage in trade. RCA for 1972 calculated from OECD STIU data bank.
Note: The technology classification is based on the OECD system.

Source: Calculated by the author from OECD (1988).

1970s), newly noncompetitive (reversals in trade and rapid rises in import penetration after 1982), at-risk competitive (showing signs of competitive disability), and competitive (consistently balanced trade and low levels of import penetration). Table 9.3 presents the 2- and 3-digit U.S. manufacturing industries according to this typology, together with the technology classification of the industry and their revealed comparative advantage in trade. This classification scheme provides a rather good fit between competitive status and the trade and import penetration indicators for each industry, but it also highlights a disturbing puzzle: the United States is (or has become) noncompetitive in several high technology industries for which it also has a comparative advantage in trade. Electronics, instruments, and office and computing machines all demonstrate both competitive distress and comparative advantage; nonelectrical machinery (a "medium technology" industry) similarly shows both competitive decline and modest comparative advantage.

While the declining competitive strength of the high technology and machinery industries has frequently been interpreted as eroding technological power, the divergence between revealed comparative advantage and competitive position indicates something else. What it suggests is a mismatch in market size, that U.S. high tech product niches do not command a large enough market volume to offset demand in products at the lower end of the industrial group. For example, U.S. imports in the instruments industry include a high proportion of consumer instruments (e.g., watches and photographic equipment), whereas exports are primarily of advanced scientific and medical instrumentation. It would be difficult to conclude that the United States has lost its technological prowess in this industry on the basis of these trade and competitive performance data; instead, the discrepancies indicate that an inability to balance markets is a key explanation of industry-level competitive disability.

The role Japan plays in the competitiveness crisis is difficult to answer because of limited empirical information—the detailed data necessary for calculating foreign market shares (country of origin of imports at the industry level) are not readily available. In terms of total manufactures trade, Japan alone has rather consistently accounted for about one-half of the deficit; Japan and the East-Asian nearly industrialized countries are the source of three-quarters of the total manufactures deficit. Some U.S. trade data do provide country of origin at the product grouping level, though, providing an indirect means of identifying key international rivals.

A crude collapsing of such product trade data into industry-level data reveals a threshold effect for Japanese imports and U.S. competitiveness. With very few exceptions, industries in which the United States is non-

Table 9.4
Relative Competitive Status of U.S. and Japanese Industries

Industry	Industries in which U.S. is competitive	Industries in which Japan is competitive
High Technology		
Instruments		X
Electronic equipment & components		X
Electrical machinery		X
Office & computing machines		X
Drugs & medicines	X	
Aerospace	X	
Medium Technology		
Motor vehicles & equipment		X
Nonelectrical machinery		X
Rubber & plastic products	X	**
Other manufacturing		
Non-ferrous metals		
Chemicals	X	
Low Technology		
Ferrous metals		X
Faricated metal products		**
Textiles, footwear, & leather		
Wood, cork, & furniture		
Stone, clay, & glass products	X	
Food, drink, & tobacco	X	
Petroleum refining	X	
Paper & printing	X	

Note: See Table 9.3 for U.S. competitive status. A Japanese industry is deemed competitive if it accounts for 25 percent or more of all imports in category as of 1987.
**Japan accounts for approximately 20 percent of imports in these industries.

competitive are also ones for which one-quarter or more of all imports are from Japan. Indeed, of the five critical industries that "explain" most of the competitiveness crisis itself (autos, electronics, textiles, electrical and nonelectrical machinery), Japan is a dominating competitor in all but textiles. Japan also accounts for roughly one-half of all imports in the instruments and office and computing machines industries, whose weakening competitive position in the 1980s has probably been the most distressing. Table 9.4 sums up the relative competitive strengths of the United States vis-a-vis Japan; U.S. competitive status is based on the typology already presented and Japan is rated as a competitor in specific industry classes if it accounts for 25 percent or more of imports in the class. What is immediately apparent is Japan's domination of the high technology industries, industries in which the United States claims to have the greatest technological and comparative advantage.

In sum, there are several key facts to concentrate on when evaluating the U.S. international competitiveness crisis. First, there does not appear to be a systematic erosion of capability throughout the industrial sector: the crisis itself is concentrated in roughly five or six manufacturing industries. Second, Japan figures as a significant competitor in virtually all U.S. industries experiencing major competitive difficulties, and consequently warrants very close scrutiny. (Note that since 1985, the U.S. trade deficit with Japan has stabilized around $60 billion and has not improved in proportion to the overall balance of trade.) Third, the coincidence of the crisis with the onset of economic recovery in 1982 could not have been fully anticipated from trade and import penetration patterns in the 1970s. While it was possible to predict worsening performance for the U.S. auto, textile, and electronics industries, the magnitude of decline in these sectors was extreme, and the erosion in the machinery, computer, and instruments industries a shock. The suddenness of the crisis suggests its roots had to be of relatively recent origin and aggravated by exchange rate and recovery effects.

Finally, the divergence between competitiveness and comparative advantage indicators for several industries hints that "unbalanced" market volume and strength may be at the root of some competitive problems. For example, Abbott (1990) finds that trade in industrial groups considered to be high tech actually capture a significant amount of low tech goods; refined definitions of high technology product classes show the United States to be doing very well in international trade. The amount of low tech "noise" masking healthy U.S. high technology performance is greatest in the electronics and instruments industries, since most imports are not (using narrow definitions) really high tech. This is an interesting consolation, but it does not mitigate the fact that the volume of U.S. high tech trade is not sufficient to offset burgeoning low tech foreign competition in electronics, instruments, and machinery—to say the least of the ongoing U.S. decline in automobiles.

TECHNOLOGY AND COMPETITIVENESS

A critical issue, from a policy and business strategy standpoint, is to better understand the role that technology plays at all levels of international

Table 9.5

Typology of Japanese Industrial R&D Performance Relative to the United States, by Industry and Competitive Status

	Competitive status of the industry	
Type of R&D Performance	Competitive	Non-competitive
Type I. Superior performance (above average on 3 or 4 R&D dimensions)	Steel Electrical machinery ** Fabricated metals	Textiles Stone and glass Nonferrous metals
Type II. Mixed performance (combination of good, poor, and/or average on R&D)	**Rubber Nonelectrical machinery Motor vehicles	Food Other transportation Chemicals
Type III. Inferior performance (well below average on 3 or 4 R&D dimensions)	Instruments Electronics	Paper and printing Pharmaceuticals

**These industries appear to be emerging competitors.

Source: Papadakis (1991).

competition, and not just high tech advantages. The patterns of competitiveness identified in the previous section provide a useful starting place, since U.S. competitive distress is concentrated in a narrow range of industries and still smaller set of countries. However, linking technology to competitiveness empirically is difficult, since by nature technology is not really a quantifiable phenomenon.

Technology is nonetheless frequently measured and usually proxied by either R&D expenditures or patenting. While this is, in many respects, an almost obscenely crude empiricism, research has repeatedly shown these measures to be usefully robust indicators of innovation and technical change. Operating on the assumption that company-funded industrial R&D bears the closest relationship to the immediate pressures of international competition, then it seems reasonable to expect that the role of technology (or technical change) in competitiveness should be reflected in the associations between R&D efforts and competitive performance. That is, the nation with the stronger industrial R&D efforts should be the more competitive.

Table 9.5 is a 3 × 2 matrix showing that, surprisingly, there is absolutely no systematic relationship between level of company-funded industrial R&D effort and competitive position. Japanese industrial R&D spending relative to the United States was analyzed for the years 1970–86 along four dimensions: the absolute volume of spending, rates of increase in R&D spending, differentials in R&D-to-sales ratios, and the rate of change in the R&D intensity of each industry. Japanese industrial R&D efforts were then rated as superior, mixed, or inferior relative to U.S. efforts, depending on their mix of scores (high, average, low) for each R&D dimension (see Table 9.6 for classification criteria). As can be seen, R&D efforts do not discriminate at all between competitive and noncompetitive Japanese manufacturing industries vis-a-vis the United States.

Japanese patenting activity in the United States likewise does not effectively differentiate competitive from noncompetitive industries (the exceptions are autos, instruments, and electronics). Patterns in the volume, rates of change, and patent productivity of R&D do not match those of competitive and noncompetitive industrial sectors; the same lack of association is also true for both Japanese R&D subsidies to industry and Japanese technology imports (Papadakis 1991). The interesting question is quite critical: if R&D and other crude measures of innovation and technology efforts do not act as indexes of competitive performance, then what differentiates competitive from noncompetitive industries?

There are two separate sets of clues that help us explain what is going on in U.S.-Japanese bilateral competitive positions. First, recent research on total factor productivity found that Japanese productivity was as high, higher, or growing faster than the United States for all of the competitive Japanese industries identified in Table 9.6 (Jorgenson and Kuroda 1988). In general, the Japanese industries that Jorgenson and Kuroda identified as having matched or exceeded U.S. levels of total factor productivity very closely duplicate those identified here with competitive advantage. Second, a comparison of industrial *basic* research expenditures shows that for all but two of the industries in which Japan is judged more competitive, their basic research efforts in the years prior to the crisis were considerably higher than the U.S. *on a dollar-per-dollar basis* and as a percentage of sales (see Table 9.6).

Table 9.6
Japanese Basic Research Efforts Relative to the United States

Competitive status of industry	Japan's basic research efforts, 1975-1981	
	Level of expenditure	Intensity index
<u>Industries in which Japan is more competitive relative to the U.S.</u>		
Electronic equipment & components inc. computers[1]	Expenditures< 50% of U.S.	.66-.75
Instruments	Expenditures< 50% of U.S.	1.4
Electrical machinery	Expenditures approx. 300% of U.S.	4.0
Motor vehicles & equipment	Expenditures approx. 300% of U.S.	4.9-3.0
Nonelectrical machinery	Expenditures approx. 200% of U.S.	3.0-4.0
Primary metals	Expenditures 100-200% of U.S.	2.0-3.0
<u>Industries in which the U.S. is more competitive relative to Japan</u>		
Aerospace	Not separately available for Japan	
Chemicals	Expenditures < 30% of U.S.	.5
Drugs & medicines	Expenditures 33-66% of U.S.	1.0
Stone, clay, & glass products	Expenditures < 30% of U.S.	less than .5
Food, drink, & tobacco	Expenditures >100% of U.S.	3.0
Petroleum refining	Expenditures < 5% of U.S.	less than .5
<u>Industries in which Japanese strength is increasing[2]</u>		
Faricated metal product	Expenditures 25-100% of U.S.	1.0
Rubber & plastic products	Expenditures 25-33% of U.S.	.75-1.0

[1] It is not possible to separate R&D data for the computer and electronics industries.
[2] Japan accounts for approximately 20 percent of imports in these industries.
Intensity index = Japanese basic research-to-net sales ratio relative to that in the United States.

Source: Papadakis (1991).

The two exceptions to this basic research preponderance are the instruments and electronics industries, although the research efforts of these two sectors clearly differentiate them from the lower basic research levels of "noncompetitive" Japanese industries. One possible explanation for the somewhat weaker relationship between patterns of basic research and competitiveness in electronics and instruments may lie in the distinctly different product mixes characterizing the U.S. and Japanese industries. The Japanese industries are dominated by consumer goods and the U.S. by more conventionally understood high tech products; it is possible that the R&D cost structures for these different product mixes are sufficiently different that Japan registers a slightly lower overall basic research spending level relative to the United States.

Strong associations between Japanese competitiveness, total factor productivity, and industrial basic research point to the significant strategic role that manufacturing technology plays in Japan and the economic advantages that it engenders. Recent research in the field of Japanese industrial political economy demonstrates that Japanese productivity advances and policies are more thorough explanators of Japanese economic performance than industrial policy per se, and that these productivity gains seem to be rooted in a fundamentally different approach to competitive strategy and manufacturing (Friedman 1988; Abegglen and Stalk 1985; Stowsky 1989; Okimoto 1989; Cohen and Zysman 1989; Johnson, Tyson, and Zysman 1989). Taken altogether, evidence on Japan's basic research investments, the technical roots of its productivity, and its competitive strategy indicate a Japanese manufacturing system that is distinctly different from others in concept, technology, and management.

MANUFACTURING TECHNOLOGY AND COMPETITIVENESS

Often overlooked in our policy analyses of technology and competitiveness is that all other factors notwithstanding (e.g., technology, industrial targeting, trade barriers, better management), economic criteria and consumer preferences are the final arbiters in the marketplace. In this regard, intense domestic competition in Japan throughout the past three decades has created a Japanese competitive strategy somewhat alien to the United States: a firm "beats out" the competition by introducing the greatest variety of any given product as cheaply and quickly as possible. To do otherwise in the high-growth environment of the Japanese economy means firm death at worst and unacceptable losses in market share at best. Lest anyone underestimate the significance of product variety, speed, and ability to appeal to the widest range of consumer tastes, Abegglen and Stalk (1985) explain how Yamaha nearly went bankrupt in the early 1980s when Honda completely replaced its motorcycle product line and introduced 81 new motorcycle models in 18 months.

U.S. business leaders have certainly understood that American companies are much slower than Japanese "at getting new ideas to market." However, the causes of U.S. debility are too narrowly attributed to managerial problems, especially regarding poor U.S. coordination of the functional interfaces of the firm (R&D, manufacturing, marketing, etc.). Behind Japan's management success is a production system that allows companies to quickly convert and retool their manufacturing base; Japanese-style management thus cannot be taken out of context from the technological core of Japanese industry. Quite simply, Japan's "organic" management style fits the technological dimensions of its manufacturing system.

So just what are these technological dimensions? Until the late 1970s, Japan's production strategy paired innovative manufacturing management with an abundance of conventional (yet customized) machinery to create flexible, "just-in-time" manufacturing systems. Multiple machining islands and serial fabrication lines were dedicated to the production of a limited range of components and subassemblies, and provided easy retooling, flexible production, and the technical basis for low (or no) internal inventory manufacturing strategies. Just-in-time production strategies cannot be underestimated for their economic advantages; when properly executed, these systems almost inevitably result in high product quality, a dramatic reduction in direct labor content, and reduction (or elimination) of inventory-induced overheads. The competitive effects of higher product quality and lower costs should be immediately apparent to even the casual analyst, but the flexibility of these systems also creates the ability to offer a wider mix of product variety and to introduce incremental change relatively quickly. To be specific, flexible manufacturing systems allow an almost dizzying array of minor variations in a defined product line, with the consequence that a broad scope of consumer tastes can be satisfied via "batch" production without any sacrifice of economies of scale.

Generally, these systems seem to work to economic advantage only in industries that lend themselves to incremental product variety and integrated sequential processing and assembly methods (autos in contrast to chemicals, for example). This is one reason why even as late as the late 1970s, Japan's international competitiveness was confined to such industries as consumer electronics, autos, and steel. American decline in these industries—uniformly attributed to poor line-of-business decisions, bad interfunctional firm management, failures to modernize, Japanese industrial policy, and a host of labor and organizational factors—cannot be understood in isolation of the very real cost, quality, and product choice advantages fostered by the manufacturing strengths of their Japanese competitors.

Understanding Japan's considerable innovations in manufacturing strategy explains why it did so well in several industries in the 1970s, but not the extraordinary burst of competitiveness it demonstrated after 1982. One additional factor is Japan's response to the first oil crisis in 1973: during the middle years of the 1970s, Japan purposefully restructured its manufacturing sector and modernized its plant and equipment to ensure maximum production efficiency. The full economic impact of these adjustments was not felt immediately by the United States because the 1978–82 recessions depressed import volumes in many industries. And, unfortunately, the U.S. manufacturing sector did not respond to the multiple oil shocks or recessions by rationalizing through modernization; instead, excess capacity was retired and product ranges narrowed to enhance economies of scale, precisely the "wrong" competitive adjustment to make during a recession for many manufacturing industries (Dumaine 1990).

Yet even this explanation does not fully capture the signficant consequences of changes in manufacturing technology that were taking place in Japan, and to this we have to account for the basic research patterns described earlier in this chapter. While Japan's industrial basic research activity in the 1970s requires further exploration, there is enough of a record to suggest that this period is characterized by a heavy emphasis on the creation and development of advanced automation systems. The magnitude and industrial location of these investments is consistent with what we know about Japan's industrial, science, and energy policies of the mid-1970s, including industry's own collaborative R&D work. Many of these policies and R&D efforts were centered on reducing the direct and indirect costs of manufacturing by creating and adopting new production equipment.

Breakthroughs in semiconductor technologies facilitated these objectives by eliminating the technical barrier to advanced automation and production machinery. Allowing the widespread physical integration of electronic microprocessors and mechanical systems, new chip technology spawned rapid innovations in such factory automation as "next generation" development of CAD/CAM, numerically controlled (NC) machine tools, robots, photo-optic sensors, and fully automated factories. Japan was as much (and still is) a pioneer in these production technologies as the United States, and even in the early 1980s was considered to be ahead of or on par with the United States in its basic research efforts (Gamota and Frieman 1988). What distinguishes Japan from the United States in the area of advanced factory automation (known as mechatronics in Japan) is its vastly superior position in the advanced development and industrial implementation of these new technologies (Gamota and Frieman 1988). The nearly exponential Japanese diffusion (beginning in roughly 1978) of nearly all of these advanced manufacturing technologies has been well documented and represents radically expanded product design and manufacturing integration, equipment flexibility, and overall system efficiency.

What seems to be clear is that on the eve of the U.S. economic recovery, the U.S. and Japanese manufacturing sectors could not have been competitively positioned more differently. Japan's highly flexible and advanced manufacturing base gave it the ability to respond rapidly to resurgent demand and satisfy a large variety of consumer tastes. The economic advantages of these world-class systems also enabled Japan to convert limited niche markets into highly profitable mass consumption, as it did, for example, with VCRs, "walkmen," and FAX machines. In contrast, U.S. economy-of-scale advantages via trimmed-down product lines were undermined by exchange rate imbalances and the greater cost efficiencies of Japanese systems. Moreover, the circumscribed product offerings of U.S. firms prevented them from exploiting all but the consumption mainstream.

TECHNOLOGY GAPS AND INTERNATIONAL COMPETITIVENESS REVISITED

Unlike previous eras, we now see a clustering of countries primed to move en masse with the next industrial wave. For these countries, trade advantage and economic development are likely to be driven by the persistent ability to succeed against foreign industries in direct product competition. The challenge of course is to understand the determinants of this sort of contemporary international competitiveness, especially with respect to the role of technology. While the jury is still out as to the actual decline in the U.S. hegemonic position since the early 1970s, the data reviewed here confirm that serious competitive problems do exist for the United States, primarily in the form of bilateral imbalances with Japan and the NICs. Japan is especially notable for the intensity and industrial breadth of its competitive ability; not only is the strength of its traditionally competitive industries (autos, electronics) increasing, but in the 1980s the scope of Japan's competitive prowess has expanded into new, and critical, manufacturing industries (machinery, instruments, semiconductors).

What exactly happened to shift the balance of competitive power so drastically—and apparently quickly—between the United States and Japan? No single factor can be an exclusive explanation, but several seem to account for changing U.S.-Japanese competitive relations. First, insights from the rather exhaustive analyses of the Japanese auto and consumer electronics industries show a persistent inability in U.S. business strategy to anticipate untapped consumer demand. From transistor radios and compact cars to VCRs and FAX machines, Japan has shown consistent skill in reducing production costs and advancing product technology in such a way that highly lucrative mass markets are created. The result of this is, as revealed in this chapter, a significant imbalance in market size between U.S. and Japanese industries with comparative advantage, an imbalance accentuated and aggravated by economic recovery and rapid growth in the new markets. U.S. high tech niches and upscale product lines (e.g., luxury cars) may enjoy comparative and technology gap advantages, but the economic gains from these markets fall far behind the mass appeal products characteristic of the "low end" of these industries.

Second, Japan's competitive strategy has created considerable innovations in manufacturing strategy, so much so that what were once merely innovations in manufacturing management now promise to transform the nature of production itself. With simultaneous emphasis on product variety, rapid responses to consumer preferences, and cost reduction, Japan's approach to competition created first a new way of organizing production and second a new generation of production technologies. As emphasized earlier, the economic trait that all of Japan's competitive industries enjoy is that of high total factor productivity, productivity rooted in manufacturing management and then reinforced by radical advances in manufacturing technology.

As Japan moves more and more heavily into high technology industries, it therefore brings with it unprecedented skills in the competitive advantage of imitation and incremental innovation. But it also demonstrates a superb ability to create new mass markets out of nascent demand, and it dominates both technological innovation and new product introductions in many areas of growing consumption. These factors, combined with Japan's industrial leadership in the development of advanced manufacturing technologies and innovative manufacturing management, present a competitor with considerable power on all dimensions of competitive strategy: imitation, innovation, manufacturing efficiency, consumer appeal, and, above all, responsiveness. Instead of concentrating on how the United States can open new technology gaps between itself and Japan, far more consideration should be given to narrowing the divergence in competitive skill that is emerging between these two nations.

REFERENCES

Abbott, Thomas A. 1990. The classification of high technology trade: A comparison of international trade administration and Bureau of Census methodologies and results. Report to the National Science Foundation, Division of Science Resources Studies.

Abegglen, James C. and George Stalk, Jr. 1985. *Kaisha, the Japanese corporation*. New York: Basic Books.

Cohen, Stephen S. and John Zysman. 1989. Diverging trajectories: Manufacturing innovation and American industrial competitiveness. In C. Johnson, L. Tyson, and J. Zysman, eds., *Politics and Productivity*. Cambridge, MA: Ballinger.

Dumaine, Brian. 1990. How to manage in a recession. *Fortune* (5 November): 58–72.

Friedman, David. 1988. *The misunderstood miracle: Industrial development and political change in Japan*. Ithaca, NY: Cornell University Press.

Gamota, George and Wendy Frieman. 1988. *Gaining ground: Japan's strides in science and technology*. Cambridge, MA: Ballinger.

Johnson, Chalmers, Laura Tyson, and John Zysman, eds. 1989. *Politics and productivity*. Cambridge, MA: Ballinger.

Jorgenson, Dale W. and Masahiro Kuroda. 1988. Productivity and international competitiveness in Japan and the United States, 1960–85. Paper prepared for the Social Science Research Council Conference on International Productivity and Competitiveness, Stanford University, 28–30 October.

OECD. 1988. The OECD compatible trade and production database. *Department of Economics and Statistics Working Papers*. Paris: OECD.

Okimoto, Daniel. 1989. *Between MITI and the market: Japanese industrial policy for high technology*. Stanford, CA: Stanford University Press.

Papadakis, Maria C. 1991. Bringing science to market: The policy implications of patterns of U.S. and Japanese science, technology, and competitiveness. Ph.D dissertation, Department of Political Science, Indiana University.

Stowsky, Jay. 1989. Trapping the benefits of technological innovation: The developmental impacts of industrial organization in the military and the marketplace. Ph.D. dissertation, Department of City and Regional Planning, University of California-Berkeley.

10 Corporate Culture in Small High Tech Firms: Lessons for Competitiveness Programs

Sally A. Rood and Andee Rappazzo

The 1980s were a decade of legislation for technology commercialization. The programs and technology transfer mechanisms being implemented as a result of these legislative initiatives involve public-private interaction. For government to work effectively with the private sector necessitates a good understanding of industry culture—particularly small firm culture. Quantitative studies of small businesses indicate that their contribution to the economy has been significant. Analysis of small business culture also reveals that small firms have characteristics that distinguish them from large corporations. Since, it is argued, organization culture is very difficult to change or control, a *greater awareness* of small firm culture on the part of government personnel will allow the government to better "read" and interact with the small high tech companies involved in commercialization programs. Enhanced understanding and dialogue will be more productive than trying to *change* industry culture to produce more "technology pull." It will permit the government to tap into those cultural characteristics that have a positive effect on competitiveness programs.

BACKGROUND

The 1980s was a decade of legislation intended to enhance U.S. competitiveness by promoting technology transfer and commercialization. A series of laws was passed to encourage spinoffs from federal laboratories, universities, and private consortia. These include:

- Stevenson-Wydler Technology Innovation Act of 1980
- Bayh-Dole University and Small Business Patent Procedures Act of 1980

- Small Business Innovation Development Act of 1982
- National Cooperative Research Act of 1984
- Federal Technology Transfer Act of 1986
- Omnibus Trade and Competitiveness Act of 1988
- National Competitiveness Technology Transfer Act of 1989
- Small Business-National Defense Laboratory Partnership Act of 1990.[1]

The major actors involved in implementing these legislative initiatives are federal agencies, universities, and industry—including both large corporations and small firms. Through examples, this chapter will provide a brief primer on small firm culture. It will argue that in writing the regulations and standards for existing technology legislation or in establishing technology-related programs to benefit American "industry," government officials need to understand more clearly small business culture in order to work together effectively with small firms through the new public-private technology transfer mechanisms.

SMALL BUSINESS: A NEW LENS FOR VIEWING CORPORATE CULTURE?

Within the high tech community, much of the emphasis on organization culture to date (in the literature, conference sessions, etc.) has focused on laboratory and university culture, and somewhat on industry culture; to an even lesser extent has the focus specifically been on small firms.

Despite popular belief in the faceless conglomerate, large organizations are often more accessible to cultural-type study than are small firms. A large company will have a public relations or marketing function in place that "speaks the language" of the researcher, and it may even have a corporate historian or policy department engaged in upholding a corporate image. Small companies can rarely afford such luxuries and rely on their personnel to retain the institutional memory. Therefore, a direct examination of small high tech companies is the most effective method to use to determine whether small companies yield useful lessons for any discussion of corporate culture as it relates to technology transfer or competitiveness.

ORGANIZATION CULTURE—THE THEORETICAL CONCEPTS

Organization culture tends to be a very subjective concept that is not easily quantified or measured. A hyperrational view of organizations that ignores cultural aspects can be onesided. There are at least two major schools of thought about the subjective concept of organization culture.

The first is a rather cognitive view where the organization is viewed as being sustained by traditions, customs, and common language. This more conservative view emerges from the literature on phenomenology (Berger and Luchmann 1966) and an interpretivist-type paradigm (Burrell and Morgan 1979), which essentially espouse that the individuals in an organization are constantly interpreting and reinterpreting the signs they get from their surroundings. This process of interpretation and reinterpretation builds up over time, according to the interpretivist perspective, such that the interpretation becomes solidified and expressed through the predictable behavior found in traditions, customs, rituals, and common language. As such, an organization begins to take on a kind of universal objective reality, even though it has been created through this process of individual subjective interpretation.

A second view of organization culture might be described as a more metaphysical approach. As with the first perspective, rituals and stories about an organization are important components of the organization's culture. However, the second view draws heavily from Jungian theory (Shelbourne 1988; Progoff 1981), which posits the existence of a collective unconscious that exists at a deeper level than what has been termed the "shared realities" of the interpretive view. At this deeper level of meaning, stories become myths; leaders become archetypes. It is this level that is referred to in the highly regarded scheme for analyzing an organization's cultural paradigm by Edgar Schein (1985). Schein's dimensions, broadly described, cover human nature and the nature of relationships (for example, cooperation vs. competition, teamwork vs. individualism, authority vs. charisma), human activity (passive vs. active), and how reality and truth are revealed in the organization—as well as assumptions in the organizations about humanity's relationship to nature (dominant, submissive). *This level of organization culture is beneath the awareness, for the most part, of the people in the organization, and hence is largely out of the realm of management control.*

CONTROL VERSUS AWARENESS

Why are the different levels and approaches to the concept of organization culture important? There are those who would argue that, with the appropriate tools, overall organization culture can be managed or changed. It is often stated and implied in the technology transfer literature and at meetings that corporate culture needs to change so that we have more "technology pull" in this country to counterbalance the current "technology push" efforts by government.

"Organization transformation" (OT) features what is called coalignment; the approach is to garner the attention of a company's employees, and to get them looking at the world in a similar manner. It is posited by some in the organization culture literature that a major function of the leader is to "create a stage" and manage symbols (Bennis and Nanus 1985; Davis 1984).

IBM and Amway are examples of large companies that have placed emphasis on managing culture and, by some standards, have achieved positive success. However, from the perspective of this chapter, this success is largely an illusion based on surface-level manipulations such as requiring a certain type of dress at work. Similarly, in terms of impacting organization culture on a superficial level, one could theoretically change the environment of an office by changing the furniture and other physical attributes. Or one could impact certain aspects of an organization's culture by changing the organization's structure or standard operating procedures (SOPs). These conscious-level aspects of organization culture are only part of the total picture; they must be considered along with unconscious-level energy.

On the other hand, unconscious organizational energy fields and metaphors with collective significance often take on a life of their own—in that sense they are "beyond control." Therefore, there are those who say organization culture, symbols, and energy forces such as archetypes can be read and tapped into but not controlled (Schein 1985).

Moreover, attempts to suppress or control these types of powerful forces could conceivably backfire—in essence, contribute to their surfacing in an unexpected manner or inopportune time. Advocates of this perspective would point out, for example, the dangers of heavy OT-type intervention in an organization, citing the possibility of instigating mob behavior, charges of mind control, mass hypnosis, and even litigation.

Thus there can be an inherent contradiction in the notion of control vis-a-vis organizational culture in the sense that attempts to control, manage, or change culture too quickly may actually contribute to an organization's downfall. Even certain of the writers favoring "planned change" have acknowledged the influence of the unconscious (Bennis 1976 and 1989), although it is not referred to as a *collective* unconscious in the Jungian sense.[2]

To illustrate how the planned change view is counter to the view being espoused in this chapter, it seems helpful to provide an example. An example could revolve around the consideration of leaders as heroes or celebrities.

One pro-planned-change writer laments the forming of cults around leaders (Bennis 1989). This chapter, on the other hand, espouses that we should recognize and accept that these circumstances exist, and that we should work with the specific situations in which they are manifested.

Thus, the simple concept of *increased awareness* of small firm culture on the part of government becomes an important part of the process of pursuing joint objectives in the arena of public-private technology transfer initiatives. This chapter will attempt to show how dialogue and communication can enhance this process.

OVERVIEW OF SOME CULTURAL FACTORS

A number of both conscious- and unconscious-level organizational factors can be studied in terms of organizational culture. These factors might include, for example, the following criteria: motivations, language, styles, organizational procedures, values, and leadership.

Much has been written about the cultural differences between industry, academia, and government with regard to *motivation*. While industry has a necessity to keep proprietary secrets, academia has a need to disseminate scientific information by publishing scholarly articles, and government has a need to make information that is publicly funded widely available.

In her colorful account of the cultural differences through her experience as the head of an industry-university consortium, Dr. Dorin Schumacher (1990) writes about the *language* difference:

each culture has a jargon of its own. I can say "P.I." or "RFP" to academics and they know instantly what I mean. I may have to qualify them, or use other words for company people. Corporate people talk about things like "ROI" which mean little, if anything, to academics. Two different languages, or else the same words meaning different things. (p. 164).

In terms of *style*, Schumacher writes: "Other cultural observations: University people arrived at the meeting when they felt like it and left when they wanted. The corporate people came at the beginning and stayed until the end of the last scheduled session. They carried out the duties we gave them faithfully" (p. 165)

Finally, Schumacher describes in interesting detail how *organizational procedures* can be so foreign to each sector:

to the industrial types ... the whole bureaucratic process of submitting a proposal to a federal agency—the awarding and managing of funds, university-sponsored programs administration, grants accounting, contracts administration, and all the bureaucratic red tape and elaborate, multi-layered accountability that go along with those things in academe—was a total unknown. So much of a mystery, in fact, they didn't even know how to ask the questions (p. 166).

Of those criteria delineating organizational culture that are noted above, only values and leadership have yet to be discussed. (Of course, there are also many other criteria that could be discussed. Those used here are only examples.) This is where an account of small firm culture—as opposed to industry, in general—can be particularly illustrative. However, before we present several small firm case studies illustrating additional cultural criteria, we will detour momentarily to describe how the nature of small business analysis to date has been largely objective—as opposed to the subjective angle inherent to organization culture studies—and quantitatively oriented.

QUANTITATIVE MEASURES OF SMALL BUSINESS

Numerous studies have described the economic and other contributions of small high tech firms in the United States. Studies and updates on the contributions of small business are sponsored regularly by the Small Business Administration's (SBA) Office of Advocacy (Scheirer 1989). According to the SBA, by 1986 almost 1 out of 4 jobs (and about 1 out of 2 new jobs) in the high tech sector were coming from small firms (Phillips 1991).

In addition, the SBA Office of Innovation, Research, and Technology annually reports on the results of the creative projects funded under the Small Business Innovation Development Act, and the General Accounting Office performs a biennial assessment of the Small Business Innovation Research program. The 1989 GAO report cited the belief by the participating agencies that their participation in the SBIR program increased likelihood that SBIR projects would lead to new inventions over other research, and that programs like SBIR increased technological innovation.

In contrast to these hopeful claims, U.S. industry is often blamed for much of the declaration that the United States is falling behind other nations economically in the competitive arena. It is said, for example, that corporate America is lethargic, that it is only focused on the bottom line of the upcoming quarter. The "NIH" (not invented here) syndrome is said to be prevalent in American companies and conglomerates.

Furthermore, as noted above, it is often argued that one reason America needs a technology push is because the level of technology pull from industry users is so minimal in this country. A 1990 survey of CEOs and

R&D directors of 275 companies, conducted by the NASA Southern Technology Applications Center, indicated apathy on the part of industry toward federal laboratory technologies due to reliance on in-house technologies, reluctance to acknowledge steps their own companies may need to make to be more competitive, and misunderstandings about technology transfer (Johnsrud et al. 1991). Only 4 percent cited federal laboratories as the sources of new technologies implemented by their companies.

This negative image of corporate America, be it true or not, does not correlate with the evidence of the contribution of small high tech firms to the U.S. economy and innovation base. The fact that most of the technology transfer legislative initiatives from the 1980s were either designed specifically for small firms or have a small business preference in them indicates that small business is considered by the U.S. Congress to be a key contributor to our economy.[3]

Using a corporate culture lens to view small high tech firms in America reveals findings that support our claim of small business as a unique entity. The appearance of, language used in, customs adhered to, symbols employed and stories told about small firms indicate that they can be quite different from the megaliths of traditional corporate America. Yet—in writing laws, establishing policies, and designing programs in this country—we often fail to take into account corporate culture as an important factor to be considered and, as a result, treat the private sector as if all companies are like IBM. The cases below describe three typical small high tech firms using a cultural lens.

SMALL FIRM EXAMPLES

A group of ten small high tech companies were visited in the summer of 1991 in order to monitor their success in the Strategic Defense Initiative's SBIR program. The companies were part of the small high tech business population included in a "success stories" video. In filming the video, access was given to all company personnel and facilities, and extensive interviews about their companies and philosophies were held with company presidents and founders. This afforded an excellent opportunity to study small companies firsthand, without disturbing the existing systems and without alerting them to our scrutiny. The company names have been changed to preserve the companies' anonymity.

Triad Corporation, in Albuquerque, New Mexico, specializes in pulse power applications. The company was initially founded in the 1970s by two scientists, but the company logo, an interlocking set of Ts, represents three partners. It was extremely important to the founders that the Supreme

Being be perceived as one of the partners in Triad's success. This belief is further encompassed in the corporate name—"tri" being the prefix for three.

The New Mexico mountains frame Triad's simple one-story building in an industrial park. Experiments are set up in a former truck garage, which is kept immaculately clean despite the dust from one of the experiments, which involves pulverizing coal. Natural light is used to its fullest extent, befitting the avocations of the scientists dressed in casual "outdoorsy" clothes. No formal laboratories exist on the premises. Only the company president, an engineer trained with an MBA and hired from another company, wears a tie and a button-down shirt. Communications between management and the work force are extremely informal; titles are not used, and there is no indication of the status of individuals. Triad now employs 23 people, of which 6 can be considered management.

Community service is an important component of what Triad believes is its unspoken pact with higher powers. The company president is the president of the local Chamber of Commerce and is active in small business advocacy on the state level. Indeed, the president was hired by one of the original company founders (the other is no longer active in company affairs) because the founder believed the president had the ability that the founder lacked to outreach to both the local social and the national technical communities.

Although scientists are assigned to a specific project, there appears to be no formal organizational structure beyond the division between what are considered "business people" (the president, the accounting department) and "lab people" (the founder, the scientists, and the technicians). As a consequence, personnel may concentrate on their assignments rather than on the political process of advancing within the organization. This may be desirable for laboratory scientists who are content to pursue their science and resist pressures from more complex organizational structures to move into management positions.

In direct contrast to the relaxed atmosphere at Triad Corporation stands the energy of Pinsuen Corporation of Taunton, Massachusetts. Although located outside of the famed Massachusetts Route 128 technology belt, Pinsuen shares the dynamic atmosphere of its northern cousins. Founded by a Chinese-American engineer who left MIT's Lincoln Laboratories, Pinsuen claims to be the number one supplier of gallium arsenide wafers (the foundation of leading edge microprocessor technology) in the United States.

The Pinsuen name comes from two Chinese words, the first meaning "quality" and the second "reliability." Quality therefore is always first and is inherent in the Pinsuen name, although only those of a Chinese culture would understand the significance. It is interesting that the names of both Triad and Pinsuen reflect values that are very important to the company founders and that are not apparent to the uninitiated in the actual reading of each name. The company name is therefore a type of secret language accessible only to the faithful.

Pinsuen is situated in a large multistory building directly off an interstate highway, and it employs 55 people. The president admits he does not need all of the space in the building but anticipates using it in the future as Pinsuen grows. As at Triad, workspaces are spacious and extremely clean.

Personnel are a little more formally dressed at Pinsuen than at Triad, but in neither case was anyone observed wearing a suit jacket. The president dresses in a shirt and tie. Scientists do wear white coats and appropriate attire where necessary. The science conducted by Pinsuen involves quality control equipment (including a clean room) that requires rigid calibration and maintenance.

The charismatic Pinsuen president is well known in the Massachusetts technology transfer community. He considers it a responsibility to educate those not knowledgeable about technology transfer, and he uses his company as an example of how to formulate licensing agreements and seek patents when he speaks at conferences. He is also well known to the financial community; Pinsuen is used by its bank as an example of the bank's investment in small business success. Bright posters depicting Pinsuen technologies, used originally for publicity purposes, were requested by the bank for display in its headquarters.

Atwater Corporation of America, located in an industrial small business park in Baltimore, Maryland, shares the atmosphere of informality of Triad and the dynamism of Pinsuen. Originally formed by two scientists working in a basement under a bank, and now standing at a work force of 20, Atwater prides itself on its working environment. Relationships are informal and flexible—the organizational structure seems to consist of the president (the other founder is no longer active in the company) and everyone else. Communication is free-flowing, and the hierarchy of personal relationships is absent from the good-natured banter that goes on between scientists, technicians, and the minimal management.

The president of Atwater can be described as a man who is hardly risk-averse. Atwater (the name is composed of the first syllable of the founders' last names—another symbol of the message relayed to "those who understand" the corporate culture) was started on the finances of the scientists' personal credit cards. To this day, the president prides himself on the company's ability to operate completely on its own money, without ever having gone to a bank or a venture capitalist for technology financing.

LESSONS FROM SMALL FIRM CULTURE

When one visits Triad, Pinsuen, and Atwater, several similarities among them leap out. The first is the existence of a charismatic leader. This characteristic is not exclusive to the small organization, as the Iacoccas of large firms do exist, but the charismatic leader of the smaller entity also operates within another similarly apparent small firm characteristic—that of the informal organizational structure.

This contrast between informal organization culture in the small company and the more formalized organization charts of the large corporation may have several implications for implementation of competitiveness legislation. Large firms may have entire departments located within an R&D organization to liaise with government; they have the resources and personnel to develop and maintain contact with technical sources. IBM, for example, is sharing Brookhaven National Laboratory's accelerator for chip design. Ray Radosevich, who has been an entrepreneur several times, has lectured and written about several advantages large firms have over small firms in technology transfer and commercialization. These include established key linkages, potential synergy with current operations, and professional management for later-stage growth.[4]

Among the small firm advantages in technology transfer and commercialization, Radosevich (1991) notes that small firms are less bureaucratic and more innovative, they have the ability to move quickly, and have little "NIH" syndrome.[5] However, small firms do have some disadvantages. On the one hand, small firms may have insight into the process of transferring technologies, but they may not have personnel available to contribute. Or they may be aware of the technical resources that exist, although they may not be aware that these resources are accessible by the small firm. This is not to say that small firms are not aware of their shortcomings in this area. Note that the founder of Triad made a special effort to recruit a president with knowledge about public organizations.

The third striking similarity among the three companies studied is the marked presence of minority personnel. Scientists/technicians may be Asian-Americans, Eastern Europeans on work visas, or African graduate students emigrating to study at local American universities. Although there is a fair preponderance of white males, even women are more prevalent than they are in traditional corporations. (Admittedly, this phenomenon may reflect the demographics of special initiatives within the scientific population as a whole.)

Minorities and women who pursue scientific careers often attribute their success to a strong internal value system that has served to overcome cultural or ethnic obstacles. This value system may be the result of social movement or perhaps of a different cultural upbringing, but it represents a strong internal conviction to certain beliefs and standards. The prevalence of minorities and foreigners may represent a preference for such value systems; it may represent a selection process by small companies of those who have the established value system that is generally built up in the close-knit upbringing of an ethnic community, or forged in the battle of overcoming common prejudices.

These individually grounded value systems may take the place of the hierarchically founded value systems (corporate quality control boards, dress codes, complicated management procedure manuals) imposed upon personnel in larger organizations. Small firm management seems to understand that loyalty to one's self, one's culture, and one's triumphs over adversity will imply loyalty to the small firm, which structures its corporate culture so that it appears to value the individual.

In summary, it appears that an analysis of small firm culture provides information on at least two criteria: value systems and structure. That is, the small firms are characterized by informal organizational structures and commonly held high values, whether the values be ethnically or socially inculturated. The presence of a charismatic leader is also of some importance, although this characteristic may be present albeit to a lesser degree in large firms that do not originate from entrepreneurial ventures.

GOVERNMENT AND SMALL FIRM ROLES

How does an understanding of small firm culture relate to the environment of the technology transfer legislation cited previously? While the 1980s were a decade of legislative changes, the early 1990s are the beginning of an era of implementation of many of these new initiatives. The issue of technology transfer enabling American competitiveness involves ensuring full understanding, compliance, and communication on the part of those organizations implementing the legislation so that the implementation phase proceeds properly. Therefore, successful implementation depends heavily upon the culture of the public and private organizations involved, and on the propensity of these organizations to understand each other.

In this era of implementation, there is a need for government officials to understand small business culture for two reasons: (1) in setting policies, standards, and regulations for the tech transfer legislation; and (2) to facilitate working with small firms on a day-to-day basis to transfer technologies and carry out legislative intent on a programmatic basis. In understanding how small business culture relates to these two purposes, it is necessary to be aware of the ways that small businesses can be involved in implementing the legislation.

As an example, through the Federal Technology Transfer Act of 1986, small firms, like large ones, can enter into cooperative R&D Agreements (CRDAs) with specific federal laboratories. The 1989 National Competitiveness Technology Transfer Act allows firms to do the same with the private-sector operators of the contractor-operated government laboratories. Similarly, the 1984 National Cooperative Research Act allows firms to join consortia of companies for conducting joint R&D.

Furthermore, the Stevenson-Wydler Technology Innovation Act of 1980 promotes the licensing of federal technologies by both small and large firms; the act establishes Offices of Research and Technology (ORTAs) to serve as a lab point of contact for industry and to market the technologies.

The Bayh-Dole University and Small Business Patent Procedures Act of 1980 allows small firms to obtain title to inventions funded by the federal government.

The Omnibus Trade and Competitiveness Act of 1988 establishes, among other things, regional centers for the transfer of manufacturing technologies to industry, including small business. It also provides for the enhancement of state-level technology extension programs that small firms can utilize.

In summary, all these programs, laws, and initiatives can involve small business as an important partner. How does an understanding of small business culture help facilitate legislative intent?

EXAMPLES OF POTENTIAL PROBLEMS TO BE AVOIDED

To answer that question, it is necessary to return to our small businesses. The charismatic leader was a common characteristic of the small businesses we studied, and we assume that the leader exists in some form in most small companies to provide entrepreneurial guidance. But in each of our studied firms, the charismatic leader empowered his following by diffusing information to that level; few secrets were kept within the small business culture. Federal or institutional implementers need to be aware that they must help company leadership to communicate programmatic intent to all levels within the small company.

It is also important for program policymakers and implementers not to create conflicts with small company values. While programs may appear "value free," they may actually imply a value imputed to large industry as a government partner in the initiative. For example, small business will not only be reluctant to participate in a CRDA that favors retention of patent rights by a larger partner, it may be incensed by a betrayal of trust that it sees as implicit in the initiative.

To exacerbate this situation, small companies talk to each other. There is a collegiality among small company owners and personnel, even within the context of fierce competition. Negotiating with a small company requires a real sense of how to structure the "deal" so that both the government and the small business win. If one small high tech company feels betrayed by the government, chances are other companies will be less apt to cooperate with the betrayers. Adherence to a strong value system within the small company often creates an allegiance to a larger value system—that is, the "inherent specialness" of all small companies.

IMPLICATIONS

This chapter draws from the literature on organization culture as well as that on technology transfer and commercialization. It began with the statement that the 1980s were "a decade of legislation" for technology commercialization. The programs and technology transfer mechanisms being implemented as a result of these legislative initiatives involve public-private interaction. For government to work effectively with the private sector necessitates a good understanding of industry culture—particularly small firm culture. Corporate culture is a basic ingredient among others (legal, economic, technical, etc.) that contributes to determining whether technology commercialization is successful or not.

We postulate that, regardless of one's view as to whether U.S. industry culture needs changing, attempting to change organization culture is not an easy thing to do. It takes a great deal of time and patience, and very skillful managers. As noted earlier, most aspects of organization culture are beneath the conscious-level awareness of those in the organization. These aspects are therefore beyond the control of management and are not directly subject to change by outside forces.

Furthermore, there are instances where it may not be advantageous to try to be so controlling as to effect change in an organization's or industry's culture. For example, the presence of a charismatic leader is an archetypical situation. It would not be wise to attempt to control or harness that particular archetypical energy because the leader's entrepreneurial nature probably had much to do with the small firm's existence in the first place. Similarly, a small firm's informal structure probably contributes to the organization's creativity and innovation. Again, to attempt to change that aspect of an organization's culture would not be advantageous to U.S. competitiveness in the long run. The presence of strong value systems and minority populations in the small firms also serves as an example of cultural characteristics that we would not want to attempt to manage or change.

Altogether the cultural characteristics observed in our tiny sample of firms provide a good example of how—instead of putting so much energy and effort into trying to *change* corporate or small firm culture so that there is more technology pull—we perhaps should put just as much energy into attempting to understand and communicate with the private sector, with particular effort necessarily placed on small firms.

Our position is that a greater awareness of small firm culture on the part of government personnel will allow the government to better "read" the small high tech companies involved in commercialization programs. Enhanced understanding will permit the government to tap into those cultural characteristics that have a positive effect on competitiveness programs.

Ironically, using a model of organization culture that assumes culture is difficult or undesirable to change fosters an environment that is more conducive to change. This is because, inherent to the metaphysical unconscious view of organization, culture is a somewhat "untraditional" view of change. This view does not consider change in the sense of cause and effect, which is based upon incentives, rewards, or punishment—or even change in the sense of control (over a situation or entity). While cause/effect implies rationality or, conversely, irrationality, this view of change implies—like the unconscious level it accompanies—nonrationality. It involves dialogue, reflexivity, and give and take, so that each party involved makes a contribution toward effecting the change. Our concluding section explains this further.

CONCLUSION

The mere presence of a corporate culture creates the necessity to ensure two-way communication between the public and private sectors specifically to negotiate the cultural differences between sectors. Therefore, the

existence of organization cultures that are difficult to change offers opportunities for intentional dialogue; it offers just the reason to require that
interaction. We cannot allow the traditional gatekeepers to be the only
avenues of communication and information exchange between government and industry where that "industry" is a small company.

Ultimately, therefore, we will need to design creative channels for
forcing that two-way communication. Because, based upon our observations, it is difficult to generalize about the hierarchical structure, language,
or procedures of small companies, we are not advocating a fixed model
for communication in all situations. The needed channels of communication should become built-in features of the new technology transfer
mechanisms such as cooperative R&D efforts between labs and companies
or consortia of companies. Similarly, we cannot focus technical personnel
exchange programs between government and industry to take place only
with larger corporate R&D labs and research departments.

Until these types of communication channels are built-in features of
programs, we must do our best to encourage multiple avenues of feedback,
interaction, and visitation. In order to continually adjust and rework
legislative intent, program policy makers and program implementers—
whether the latter be in federal or state governments, universities, or other
institutions—must keep in constant contact with the small companies with
which they are *directly* working. At the very least and on a more general
basis, communication patterns will benefit from increased involvement
with trade and professional societies for small firms.

NOTES

1. In addition to existing legislation, pending legislative initiatives (e.g., the
American Technology Preeminence Act of 1991) will call for increased interaction between federal personnel and small firms. At the state level as well, states
are establishing programs in response to small business technology requirements.

2. Bennis, for example, has updated his earlier (1976) book, *The Unconscious Conspiracy: Why Leaders Can't Lead,* with a version entitled *Why
Leaders Can't Lead: The Unconscious Conspiracy Continues* (1989). In the
Preface he writes: "The book is not overly optimistic. But I do think change is
possible—even change for the better" (p. xiii). He does not acknowledge the
importance of uncontrollable unconscious forces, and focuses again on superficial aspects of taking charge by offering specific suggestions for keeping a
routine, for example, or countering turmoil and inertia.

3. Furthermore, the purpose of some of the most recent legislation and
federal programs is to fund or strengthen the role of state and local government

economic development and technical assistance programs. These programs can serve as intermediaries in performing outreach for deferral laboratories or identification of local small firms for greater involvement in the technology transfer programs.

4. Additional economic and technical advantages of large firms cited by Radosevich, but not the subject of this chapter, include market power, access to capital markets, better protection of proprietary technology positions, the ability to absorb large fixed transaction costs, and technical capacity.

5. Small firm advantages in technology commercialization also include the economic advantage of lower cost of operations and that they are more efficient job and wealth creators.

REFERENCES

Bennis, Warren. 1976. *The unconscious conspiracy: Why leaders can't lead.* New York: American Management Association.

———. 1989. *Why leaders can't lead: The unconscious conspiracy continues.* San Francisco: Jossey-Bass.

——— and Burt Nanus. 1985. *Leaders: The strategies for taking charge.* New York: Harper & Row.

Berger, Peter L. and Thomas Luckmann. 1966. *The social construction of reality: A treatise in the sociology of knowledge.* Garden City, NY: Doubleday.

Burrell, Gibson and Gareth Morgan. 1979. *Sociological paradigms and organizational analysis: Elements of the sociology of corporate life.* Portsmouth, NH: Heinemann Educational Books.

Davis, Stanley M. 1984. *Managing corporate culture.* Cambridge, MA: Ballinger.

Johnsrud, Cristy, J. Ronald Thornton, and Thomas Horak. 1991. *National technology transfer center (NTTC) commercial user needs assessment survey: Report of survey findings.* Alachua, FL: Southern Technology Applications Center.

Phillips, Bruce D. 1991. "The increasing role of small firms in the high technology sector: Evidence from the 1980s." *Business Economics*, January: 40–47.

Progoff, Ira. 1981. *Jung's psychology and social meaning: A comprehensive statement of C. G. Jung's psychological theories and an interpretation of their significance for the social sciences.* New York: Dialogue House Library.

Radosevich, Ray. 1991. "New business development from New Mexico's federal labs." Presentation at the conference, Technology Commercialization: Innovative Alliances for Economic Development. Albuquerque, 12–13 September.

Schein, Edgar H. 1985. *Organizational culture and leadership: A dynamic view.* San Francisco: Jossey-Bass.

Scheirer, William K. 1989. "The population and birth rates of high technology firms, 1976–1986." Office of Advocacy. U.S. Small Business Administration, 31 March.

Schumacher, Dorin. 1990. "Cultural differences in the R&D consortium: Meeting the management challenge." In Robert W. Harrison, ed., *Technology Transfer in a Global Economy: Proceedings of the Technology Transfer Society 15th Annual Meeting*, 26–28 June, Dayton, Ohio, pp. 163–167.

Shelbourne, Walter A. 1988. *Mythos and logos in the thought of Carl Jung: The theory of the collective unconscious in scientific perspective.* Albany, NY: State University of New York Press.

U.S. General Accounting Office. 1989. *Federal research: Assessment of small business innovation research programs.* GAO/RCED-89-39.

Selected Bibliography

Abegglen, James C. and George Stalk, Jr. 1985. *Kaisha, the Japanese corpora-tion.* New York: Basic Books.

Arrow, Kenneth. 1962. Economic welfare and the allocation of resources for invention. In R. Nelson, ed., *The Rate and Direction of Inventive Activ-ity.* Princeton, NJ: Princeton University Press.

Arthur, W. Brian. 1989. Competing technologies, increasing returns, and lock-in by historical events. *Economic Journal* 99: 116–131.

Atkinson, Robert D. 1988. *State programs for technology development.* Report of the National Association of State Development Agencies (April).

———. 1991. Some states take the lead: Explaining reformation of state tech-nology policies. *Economic Development Quarterly* 5 (February).

Babbitt, Bruce. 1984. The states and the reindustrialization of America. *Issues in Science and Technology* (Fall).

Barnett, Homer. 1953. *Innovation: The basis of cultural change.* New York: McGraw-Hill.

Bennis, Warren. 1976. *The unconscious conspiracy: Why leaders can't lead.* New York: American Management Association.

———. 1989. *Why leaders can't lead: The unconscious conspiracy continues.* San Francisco: Jossey-Bass.

——— and Burt Nanus. 1985. *Leaders: The strategies for taking charge.* New York: Harper & Row.

Berger, Peter L. and Thomas Luckmann. 1966. *The social construction of reality: A treatise in the sociology of knowledge.* Garden City, NY: Doubleday.

Bertsch, Gary K., Heinrich Vogel, and Jan Zielonka, eds. 1991. *After the revolution: East-West trade and technology transfer.* Boulder, CO: Westview Press.

Bloch, Erich. 1986. *Basic research: The key to economic competitiveness.* Washington, DC: National Science Foundation. NSF-86–21.

Bozeman, Barry and Michael Crow. 1990. The environments of U.S. R&D laboratories: political and market influences. *Policy Sciences* 23: 25–56.

———. 1991. Technology transfer from U.S. government and university R&D laboratories. *Technovation* 11(4): 231–246.

Brander, James. 1988. Rationales for strategic trade and industrial policy. In Paul Krugman, ed., *Strategic trade policy and the new international economics.* Cambridge, MA: MIT Press, pp. 23–46.

Bromley, D. Allan. 1990. *U.S. technology policy.* Washington, DC: Executive Office of the President.

Brooks, Harvey and Lewis Branscomb. 1989. Rethinking the military's role in the economy. *Technology Review* (August-September): 54–64.

Burrell, Gibson and Gareth Morgan. 1979. *Sociological paradigms and organizational analysis: Elements of the sociology of corporate life.* Portsmouth, NH: Heinemann Educational Books.

Carnegie Commission on Science, Technology and Government. 1990. *New thinking and American defense technology.* New York: Carnegie Commission.

Chapman, Robert E., Marianne K. Clarke, and Eric Dobson. 1990. *Technology-based economic development: A study of state and federal technical extension services.* Gaithersburg, MD: National Institute of Standards and Technology. NIST Special Publication 786.

Cohen, Linda and Roger Noll. 1991. *The technology pork barrel.* Washington, DC: Brookings Institution.

Council on Competitiveness. 1991. *Gaining new ground: Technology priorities for America's future.* Washington, DC: Council on Competitiveness.

Crow, Michael and Barry Bozeman. 1987. A new typology for R&D laboratories: implications for policy analysis. *Journal of Policy Analysis and Management* 6: 328–341.

Crow, Michael, Mark Emmert, and Carol Jacobson. 1990. Government-supported industrial research institutes in the United States. *Policy Studies Journal* (Fall): 59–74.

Dasgupta, Partha. 1987. The economic theory of technology policy: an introduction. In Partha Dasgupta and Paul Stoneman, eds., *Economic theory and technological performance.* Cambridge: Cambridge University Press, p. 723.

David, Paul. 1985. New standards for the economics of standardization. In Partha Dasgupta and Paul Stoneman, eds., *Economic theory and technological performance.* Cambridge: Cambridge University Press, pp. 206–239.

Davis, Stanley M. 1984. *Managing corporate culture.* Cambridge, MA.: Ballinger.

Dertouzos, Michael, Richard Lester, Robert Solow, and the MIT Commission on Industrial Productivity. 1989. *Made in America*. Cambridge, MA: MIT Press.

Doctors, Samuel I. 1969. *The role of federal agencies in technology transfer*. Cambridge, MA: MIT Press.

Downs, George B. and L. B. Mohr. 1967. Conceptual issues in the study of innovation. *Administrative Science Quarterly* 21 (December): 700–714.

Eads, George and Richard Nelson. 1971. Government support of advanced civilian technology: Power reactors and the supersonic transport. *Public Policy* 19: 405–428.

Emery, E. F. and E. L. Trist. 1978. The causal texture of organizational environments. In James M. Shafritz and Phillip H. Whitbeck, eds., *Classics of organization theory*. 1965 reprint, Oak Park, IL: Moore Publishing Co.

Ergas, Henry. 1987. Does technology policy matter? In Bruce Guile and Harvey Brooks, eds., *Technology and global industry*. Washington, DC: National Academy of Engineering, pp. 191–245.

Ezra, Arthur. 1975. Technology utilization: Incentives and solar energy. *Science* 28 (February): 707–713.

Feller, Irwin. 1986. Research and technology transfer linkages in agriculture. In Lawrence Busch and William Lacy, eds., *The agricultural scientific enterprise: A system in transition*. Boulder, CO: Westview Press, pp. 280–295.

Forrer, John. 1989. *State competitive research grant programs*. Washington, DC: National Governors' Association and National Science Foundation.

Freeman, Christopher. 1987. *Technology policy and economic performance*. London: Pinter Publishers.

Friedman, David. 1988. *The misunderstood miracle: Industrial development and political change in Japan*. Ithaca, NY: Cornell University Press.

Furash, Edward E. 1971. The problem of technology transfer. In R. A. Bauer and K. J. Gergen, eds., *The study of policy formation*. New York: The Free Press.

Gabor, Dennis. 1970. *Innovations: Scientific, technological, and social*. New York: Oxford University Press.

Gamota, George and Wendy Frieman. 1988. *Gaining ground: Japan's strides in science and technology*. Cambridge, MA: Ballinger.

Gomory, Ralph E. and Roland W. Schmitt. 1988. Science and product. *Science* (May): 1131–1132.

Goodman, Seymour E., Marjory S. Blumenthal, and Gary L. Geipal. 1989–90. Export controls reconsidered. *Issues in Science and Technology* 6 (Winter): 40–44.

Government-University-Industry Research Roundtable, National Governors' Association, and National Research Council. 1987. *State government strategies for self-assessment of science and technology programs for economic development*. Washington, DC: National Academy Press.

Grossman, Gene. 1988. Strategic export promotion: A critique. In Paul Krugman, ed., *Strategic trade policy and the new international economics.* Cambridge, MA: MIT Press, pp. 47-68.

Havelock, Ronald. 1969. *Planning for innovation through dissemination and utilization of knowledge.* University of Michigan, Center for the Utilization of Scientific Knowledge.

Hough, Granville W. 1977. *Technology diffusion: Federal programs and procedures.* Mt. Airy, MD: Lomond Books.

Ikenberry, Stanley O. and R. C. Friedman. 1972. *Beyond academic departments: The story of institutes and centers.* San Francisco: Jossey-Bass.

Johnson, Chalmers, Laura Tyson, and John Zysman, eds. 1989. *Politics and productivity.* Cambridge, MA: Ballinger.

Lambright, W. Henry. 1976. *Governing science and technology.* New York: Oxford University Press.

———. and Dianne Rahm. 1991. Science, technology and the states. *Forum for Applied Research and Public Policy* 6(3): 49–60.

Lambright, W. Henry and Albert Teich. 1976. Technology transfer as a problem in interorganizational relationships. *Administration and Society* 8: 29–54.

———. 1989. Science, technology, and state economic development. *Policy Studies Journal* 18 (Fall): 135–147.

Levine, Arthur. 1989. Space technology and state competitiveness. *Policy Studies Journal* 18 (Fall): 148–163.

Lyons, Bruce. 1987. International trade and technology policy. In Partha Dasgupta and Paul Stoneman, eds., *Economic theory and technological performance.* Cambridge: Cambridge University Press, pp. 168–205.

Mansfield, E. 1980. Basic research and productivity increase in manufacturing. *American Economic Review* 70: 863–873.

Marcus, Alan. 1985. *Agricultural science and the quest for legitimacy.* Ames: Iowa State University Press.

———. 1986. From state chemistry to state science: The transformation of the idea of the agricultural experiment station, 1875–1887. In Lawrence Busch and William Lacy, eds., *The agricultural scientific enterprise: A system in transition.* Boulder, CO: Westview Press, pp. 3–12.

Minnesota, Department of Trade and Economic Development. 1988. *State technology programs in the United States: 1988.* Report by the Office of Science and Technology, July.

Morgan, Steve. 1991. Director of Space Industries, Virginia Center for Innovative Technology. Herndon, Virginia. Telephone interview, 16 April.

Mowery, David. 1983. Economic theory and government technology policy. *Policy Sciences* 16: 27–43.

———. and Nathan Rosenberg. 1989. *Technology and the pursuit of economic growth.* Cambridge: Cambridge University Press.

Murrin, Thomas J. 1990. Thinking globally, acting nationally. *Issues in Science and Technology* 6 (Summer): 50–54.

National Academy of Sciences. 1987. *Balancing the national interest: U.S. national security export controls and global economic competitiveness* (known as the Allen Report). Washington, DC: National Academy Press.

————, National Academy of Engineering, Institute of Medicine. 1991. *Finding common ground: U.S. export controls in a changed global environment.* Washington, DC: National Academy Press.

National Governors' Association. 1983. *Technology and growth: State initiatives in technology innovation.* Final Report of the Task Force on Technological Innovation, October.

National Science Foundation. 1983. *The process of technological innovation: Reviewing the literature.* Washington, DC: National Science Foundation.

————. 1984. Experimental Program to Stimulate Competitive Research (EPSCoR) Program Plan FY 1985 (November 19).

————. 1988. EPSCoR Science and Technology Action Plan FY 1989, draft report, 15 October.

————. 1991. *Benefits of basic research.* Washington, DC: National Science Foundation.

National Space Council. 1991. *U.S. commercial space policy guidelines.* Washington, DC: National Space Council.

Nelson, Richard. 1959. The simple economics of basic scientific research. *Journal of Political Economy* 67 (3): 297–306.

————. 1988. Institutions supporting technical change in the U.S. In Giovanni Dosi, Christopher Freeman, Richard Nelson, Gerald Silverberg, and Luc Soete, eds., *Technical change and economic theory.* London: Pinter Publishers, pp. 312–329.

————, Merton Peck, and Edward Kalachek. 1967. *Economic growth and public policy.* Washington, DC: RAND Corporation and Brookings Institution.

Nelson, Richard and Sidney Winter. 1977. In search of a useful theory of innovation. *Research Policy* 6: 36–77.

Oklahoma Center for the Advancement of Science and Technology. 1988a. *OCAST program update: A status report on programs.* Oklahoma City: Oklahoma Center for the Advancement of Science and Technology.

————. 1988b. *Oklahoma Centers of Excellence Program 1989 program solicitation.* Oklahoma City: Oklahoma Center for the Advancement of Science and Technology.

Osborne, David. 1988. *Laboratories of democracy.* Boston: Harvard Business School Press.

————. 1990. Refining state technology programs. *Issues in Science and Technology* (Summer): 55–61.

Phelps, Paul B. and Paul R. Brockman. 1992. *Science and technology programs in the states 1992.* Alexandria, VA: Advanced Development Distribution, Inc.

Quigley, John. 1982. Residential construction. In Richard Nelson, ed., *Government and technical progress.* New York: Pergamon Press, pp. 361–410.

Rahm, Dianne. 1989. Federal efforts to enhance U.S. competitiveness: The encouragement of domestic cooperation. *Policy Studies Journal* 18 (1): 89–99.

————. 1990. Clearing the way for cooperative R&D: Policies that promote industry-university-government cooperation. In Tarek Khalil and Bulent Bayraktar, eds., *Technology Management II.* Norcross, GA: Industrial Engineering and Management Press, pp. 327–334.

Rahm, Dianne, Barry Bozeman, and Michael Crow. 1988. Technology transfer and competitiveness: An empirical assessment of the roles of university and government research and development labs. *Public Administration Review* 48 (6): 969–978.

Rahm, Dianne and Thomas F. Luce, Jr. 1992. Issues in the design of state science- and technology-based economic development programs: The case of Pennsylvania's Ben Franklin partnership. *Economic Development Quarterly* 6 (1): February 41–51.

Reich, Robert B. 1989. The quiet path to technological preeminence. *Scientific American* (October): 41–47.

————. 1990–91. Does corporate nationality matter? *Issues in Science and Technology* 6 (Winter): 40–44.

Reimann, Curt W. 1989. The Baldrige award: Leading the way in quality initiatives. *Quality Progress* (July): 35–39.

Research and Policy Committee. 1986. *Leadership for dynamic state economies.* New York: Committee for Economic Development.

Rice, Sherry C. 1990. Technology management as an alliance issue: A review of the literature. *Washington Quarterly* 13 (Winter): 219–235.

Roessner, J. David. 1984. Commercializing solar technology: The government role. *Research Policy* 13: 235–246.

Rogers, E. M. 1983. *Diffusion of innovations.* New York: Free Press.

———— and F. Shoemaker. 1971. *Communication of innovation,* 2d ed. New York: Free Press.

Rosenberg, Charles. 1964. The Adams Act: Politics and the cause of scientific research. *Agricultural History* 38: 3–12.

————. 1971. Science, technology, and economic growth: The case of the agricultural experiment station scientist, 1875–1914. *Agricultural History* 45: 1–20.

Ruttan, Vernon and Yujiro Hayami. 1984. Toward a theory of induced institutional innovation. *Journal of Development Studies* 20: 203–223.

Schankerman, Mark. 1990. Review of *Economic policy and technological performance,* edited by Partha Dasgupta and Paul Stoneman. *Journal of Economic Literature* 28: 1759–1761.

Schein, Edgar H. 1985. *Organizational culture and leadership: A dynamic view.* San Francisco: Jossey-Bass.

Scherer, Frederic. 1965. Government research and development programs. In Robert Dorfman, ed., *Measuring benefits of government investments.* Washington, DC: Brookings Institution, pp. 12–57.

Schmandt, Jurgen and Robert Wilson, eds. 1987. *Promoting high-technology industry: Initiatives and policies for state governments.* Boulder, CO: Westview Press.

Scott, Roy. 1970. *The reluctant farmer.* Urbana: University of Illinois Press.

Shapira, Philip. 1990. *Modernizing manufacturing: New policies to build industrial extension services.* Washington, DC: Economic Policy Institute.

Shelbourne, Walter A. 1988. *Mythos and logos in the thought of Carl Jung: The theory of the collective unconscious in scientific perspective.* Albany: State University of New York Press.

Shinn, Allen, M. Jr. 1990. Science, technology, and free speech. *Issues in Science and Technology* 6 (Summer): 28–31.

Tassey, Gregory. 1990a. *The functions of technology infrastructure in a competitive economy.* Gaithersburg, MD: National Institute of Standards and Technology.

————. 1990b. *Investment in quality and U.S. competitiveness.* Gaithersburg, MD: National Institute of Standards and Technology.

Tonelson, Alan. 1991. What is the national interest? *The Atlantic* (268): 35–52.

Tornatsky, Louis G. et al. 1983. *The process of technological innovation: Reviewing the literature.* Washington, DC: National Science Foundation.

Twiss, Brian. 1986. *Managing technology and innovation*, 3d ed. New York: Pittman Publishers.

U.S. Department of Commerce, Technology Administration. 1990. *Emerging technologies: A survey of technical and economic opportunities.* Washington, DC: U.S. Department of Commerce.

U.S. Department of Defense. 1991. *The Department of Defense Critical Technologies Plan.* Washington, D.C.: U.S. Department of Defense.

Wallerstein, Michael B. with William W. Snyder, Jr. 1991. The evolution of U.S. export control policy: 1949–1989. In *Finding common ground*, Washington DC: National Academy Press.

White, Lawrence. 1982. The motor vehicle industry. In Richard Nelson, ed., *Government and technical progress.* New York: Pergamon Press, pp. 411–440.

Wolf, Charles. 1988. *Markets or governments.* Cambridge, MA: MIT Press.

Index

About the Contributors

JAMES A. BALL is a Program Manager for Technology Development with Systems Engineering and Management Associates. A retired Air Force Colonel, he is the former Director of Technology Applications for the Strategic Defense Initiative Office.

BRACK BROWN is an Associate Professor of Government and Politics at George Mason University. His basic research concerns are with administrative and policy development through innovation and technology transfer. Dr. Brown has tracked such developments in Africa, Eastern Europe, and the United States.

ROBERT E. CHAPMAN is a Senior Economist with the Office of Quality Programs in the National Institute of Standards and Technology, where he manages the Malcolm Baldrige National Quality Award Program. Dr. Chapman led technical projects in the areas of model evaluation, software engineering, and the development of standardized economic methods for evaluating alternative engineering system designs.

IRWIN FELLER is Director of the Graduate School of Public Policy and Administration and a Professor in the Department of Economics at Pennsylvania State University. His research has centered around the economics of technology policy, the diffusion of innovations, university-industry-government R&D partnerships, the evaluation of state technology programs, and U.S.-European Economic Community strategies for employing R&D funding as a regional economic growth stimulus.

W. HENRY LAMBRIGHT is a Professor of Political Science and Public Administration at the Maxwell School, Syracuse University. He is also Director of the Science and Technology Policy Center of Syracuse Research Corporation. Dr. Lambright has authored numerous books and articles on topics such as presidential management of technology, NASA, technology transfer, innovative public management, and governing science and technology.

ARTHUR L. LEVINE is a Professor of Public Administration at Baruch College, City University of New York. He is the author of numerous works on space policy and management.

MARK J. O'GORMAN is a Ph.D. candidate in Political Science at the Maxwell School, Syracuse University. His specializations are in U.S. public policy, public administration, and science policy.

MARIA PAPADAKIS is an Assistant Professor of Public Administration and a Senior Research Associate in the Technology and Information Policy Program at Syracuse University's Maxwell School. Dr. Papadakis has also been a visiting researcher at Japan's National Institute for Science and Technology, a technology analyst at NSF, and an international trade analyst at the U.S. International Trade Commission. Her research concerns the impact of science and technology on international trade and competitiveness.

LINDA E. PARKER is a Program Analyst with the National Science Foundation's program evaluation staff. She studies the impact and efficacy of NSF's programs and various facets of the relationship between federal research support and university research management.

DIANNE RAHM is an Assistant Professor of Government and International Affairs at the University of South Florida. Her research has focused on federal and state policies that affect scientific and technological change, technology transfer, economic development, and competitiveness.

ANDEE RAPPAZZO currently supports the Strategic Defense Initiative's Small Business Innovation Research program. She concentrates her research on small businesses and their reaction to industrial and technology policy.

CURT W. REIMANN is the Director of the Office of Quality Programs at the National Institute of Standards and Technology. Dr. Reimann has also served as Director of the National Measurement Laboratory, which is responsible for developing and maintaining the nation's basic physical, chemical, and radiation measurements and standards.

SALLY A. ROOD is a Manager of Technology Information Services for Systems Engineering and Management Associates. She currently provides assistance to the Technology Administration at the Department of Commerce, the Federal Laboratory Consortium, and the Technology Applications program at the Strategic Defense Initiative. Ms. Rood has also worked for a number of other government organizations, including the National Association of Counties, the U.S. Economic Development Administration, the National Council for Urban Economic Development, the Academy for State and Local Governments, and the U.S. Conference on Mayors.

ALBERT H. TEICH is Director of Science and Policy Programs at the American Association for the Advancement of Science (AAAS). Dr. Teich has also been head of the AAAS Office for Public Sector Programs and a manager of science policy studies. Prior to joining AAAS, Dr. Teich was Deputy Director of the Graduate Program in Science, Technology and Public Policy at George Washington University. The author of numerous books and articles, his major research interests are in science, technology, and society with a special emphasis on public policymaking and budgetary politics.

Policy Studies Organization publications issued with Greenwood Press /
Quorum Books

Implementation and the Policy Process: Opening up the Black Box
Dennis J. Palumbo and Donald J. Calista, editors

Policy Theory and Policy Evaluation: Concepts, Knowledge, Causes, and Norms
Stuart S. Nagel, editor

Biotechnology: Assessing Social Impacts and Policy Implications
David J. Webber, editor

Public Administration and Decision-Aiding Software: Improving Procedure and
Substance
Stuart S. Nagel, editor

Outdoor Recreation Policy: Pleasure and Preservation
John D. Hutcheson, Jr., Francis P. Noe, and Robert E. Snow, editors

Conflict Resolution and Public Policy
Miriam K. Mills, editor

Teaching Public Policy: Theory, Research, and Practice
Peter J. Bergerson, editor

The Reconstruction of Family Policy
Elaine A. Anderson and Richard C. Hula, editors

Gubernatorial Leadership and State Policy
Eric B. Herzik and Brent W. Brown, editors

Public Policy Issues in Wildlife Management
William R. Mangun, editor

Health Insurance and Public Policy: Risk, Allocation, and Equity
Miriam K. Mills and Robert H. Blank, editors

Public Authorities and Public Policy: The Business of Government
Jerry Mitchell, editor